D0906088

Elite Oral History
Discourse

STUDIES IN RHETORIC AND COMMUNICATION
General Editors:
E. Culpepper Clark
Raymie E. McKerrow
David Zarefsky

Hear O Israel:
The History of American Jewish Preaching, 1654–1970
Robert V. Friedenberg

A Theory of Argumentation
Charles Arthur Willard

Elite Oral History Discourse:
A Study of Cooperation and Coherence
Eva M. McMahan

Eva M. McMahan

Elite Oral History Discourse
A Study of Cooperation and Coherence

Foreword by
Ronald J. Grele

The University of Alabama Press   Tuscaloosa and London

Copyright © 1989 by
The University of Alabama Press
Tuscaloosa, Alabama 35487
All rights reserved
Manufactured in the United States of America

Portions of this book have appeared in slightly different
form in *Oral History Review* 15 (Spring 1987): 185–208,
as "Speech and Counter Speech: Language-in-use in
Oral History Fieldwork."

Library of Congress Cataloging-in-Publication Data

McMahan, Eva M.
    Elite oral history discourse : a study of cooperation and
coherence / Eva M. McMahan.
        p.   cm. — (Studies in rhetoric and communication)
    Bibliography: p.
    Includes index.
    ISBN 0–8173–0437–1
    1. Oral history.   I. Title.   II. Series.
D16.14.M35   1989
902'.8—dc19   88-36913
                                                            CIP

British Library Cataloguing-in-Publication Data available

This book
is dedicated to my parents,
Helen Gillespie McMahan and
Everett Lee McMahan,
who instilled in me
the value of becoming educated
and who generously
supported me
in pursuit of that goal.

Contents

Foreword

Each year millions of Americans either are interviewed or interview someone. When one thinks of the total of employment interviews, talk show guests, man-on-the-street interviews, social and marketing surveys, or cultural criticism in the form, it is overwhelming to think about just how much information is conveyed through and by interviews in our culture. In many of these interviews detailed historical information is collected, people are asked about the past and their experiences in the past, but usually in an offhand manner or as background information to the main topic. Only a few of this massive number of interviews can rightly be called oral history interviews—interview sessions in which both interviewer and interviewee sit down consciously to collect a memoir of the history of some lived event.

Each interview genre has its own form and its own meaning. Each is special in this way. What is so special about the oral history interview is the meaning it derives from the role of history in our culture. An oral history interview is "for the record." It is "for the ages," "for scholars." It is fraught with social and cultural significance. For some reason, when people are asked to give an oral history interview it takes on a seriousness, a sense of purpose that other conversations do not have. History for most Americans is a responsible project. Not only is the interviewee being called upon to recollect what happened, but we are also being called upon to give that recollection meaning, to put it into some context, to interpret the event, to try to be self-critical. The oral history interview is a complex event. Not only is it the construction of a text, the creation of an autobiography, a "life as narrative" as Jerome Bruner has called it,[1] but it is also a social event. As such it reflects the social relations of the moment—those between interviewer and interviewee—and those of the larger culture—academic and citizen, for instance, or teacher and student, grandmother and grandson, depending upon the status and role of the interviewer and interviewee. It is also a medium through which the interviewee addresses the community and its past. To create a record of one's life for future generations is to construct a document of the culture and that construction is a complicated process. It is the illumination of that region of the mind where, as Alice Kessler Harris has noted, "memory, myth, ideology, language, and historical cognition interact in a dialectical transformation of the word into a historical artifact."[2]

In our work in oral history, for many years, we worked rather with commonsense theories and commonsense social skills that were married to a traditional historical training. If we looked to other disciplines or other interviewers, it was to journalism and jounalists. Relations with other social science fieldworkers were tentative, tangential. In recent years all of that has changed as oral historians have begun to explore methodologies and as fieldworkers in folklore, anthropology, and sociology have turned their attention to oral history. Anthropologists such as Sidney Mintz and Francoise Morin, folklorists such as Charles Joyner and Roger Abrahams, and sociologists such as Paul Thompson and Charles Kaplan have enriched our discussions of what it is we do when we conduct an oral history interview, and they have put that work within a larger set of traditions in the social sciences.[3] Some of the most stimulating of this work has been done by Eva McMahan and her colleagues in their attempt to understand the oral history interview as a communicative event and speech act.[4] Merging the concerns of communication theory and philosophical hermeneutics, they first alerted oral historians to the complex struggle for meaning taking place within an interview and offered a method whereby we can understand the transformations that take place during that struggle. Their goal was, they said, to use the study of communicative performance and the understanding of hermeneutics to lead us to "a systematic understanding of the oral history interview."[5] In this volume, Eva McMahan takes up that mission. It is a unique work. It brings to our discussion the theories and language of communication, and at the same time it respects the special nature of the oral history interview and the special nature of the relationships contained in the interview. For convenience and clarity it begins with a discussion of elite interviewing, a situation in which the similarity between the oral historian and the interviewee is clear in their general agreement on the usefulness of history and in which there is a shared vision of historical process and causality.

This book is also unique because in it the author examines in some detail actual interviews conducted by a number of oral historians working on a number of projects. It is the first such work that comes to my mind. Here we can see the process of the interview as it actually emerges in the event itself. It is, of course, as McMahan points out, a work that relies on transcripts and audiotapes rather than on videotapes and in that sense is limited in what can be observed and analyzed. Unfortunately, in a written medium there are few alternatives, and because few programs systematically videotape such lengthy interviews, the visual dimension of the social situation is unavailable to us. Still, we must begin somewhere and McMahan's book raises the discussion of our work to new and more complex levels of analysis and generalization. Serious students of oral history welcome this volume.

Ronald J. Grele

Preface

Over the past thirty years, oral history has found increasing favor among social scientists and humanists. Works such as T. Harry Williams's biography of Huey Long, Studs Terkel's "memory books" of the Great Depression and of World War II, David Halberstam's search for the roots of American foreign policy in the culture of the political elite, Howell Raines's history of the civil rights movement, and Alex Haley's tour de force with *Roots* have popularized oral investigatory techniques and helped to illustrate some of its pathbreaking potential.

Likewise, scholars such as Daniel Bertaux, writing about life history and sociology; Philippe Joutard, discussing "ethnotexts"; Francoise Morin, explaining the use of life history in anthropology; and Bronslaw Mitztal, writing about oral history and socio-historical knowledge, have "rediscovered" the oral interview as a valuable method for obtaining information about the cultural realities and historical consciousness of people that can be expressed in the form of autobiography, biography, ethnotexts, and life history. As a result, the oral interview method is once again the subject of debate about its merit as a tool for gathering data about people, their histories, and their culture. One of the issues under discussion is the question of how the communicative performances of interviewer and interviewee jointly influence the production of the audio, video, and written records of the interview. As David Henige pointedly observes in his recent book *Oral Historiography*, our fieldwork experiences as oral historians force us to recognize the "transactional" nature of the interview method in which the face-to-face interaction involved in oral interviews affects the nature of the materials obtained.

The purpose of this book is to shed light on the communicative experience of oral history interviewing, the transactional process of which Henige speaks. By oral history, I mean interviews/conversations designed to record the memorable experiences of people. This book, which is written for the scholar/practitioner of oral history, is about the questions and answers used by oral historians and respondents as they jointly create cooperative, coherent accounts of memorable lived-through experiences. Specifically, I am interested in describing the principles of conversational production that account for the production of cooperative, coherent discourse in interviews with elites. The term *elite* refers to James Wilkie's distinction between elite and nonelite members of society. The elites, Wilkie says, are those persons who develop a lore that justifies their attempts to control society. The nonelites, on the other hand, are those persons who create a lore to explain their lack of control. The data upon which this book is based, therefore, are audiotapes and transcriptions of interviews with American male elites. These types of interviews have been chosen as the starting point for my ongoing descriptive research program because interviews with elite informants reflect a large proportion of extant records and because I want to reduce the number of variables impacting the communicative performances. Thus the work reported here is the first in a series of studies that eventually will include sociocultural variables such as age, gender, class, nationality, ethnic origin, and race.

I have two reasons for writing this book. I believe that examination of the relationship between the *process* of oral history interviewing and the *product* of the interview—the oral text—is needed. Just as full appreciation of a symphony emerges both from the act of listening to a particular rendition of the score and from an awareness of the creative elements that contribute to the rendition, so full understanding of the nature of the oral text develops both from examining the oral text and from analyzing the oral interview process that creates the product. In addition, I believe that communication theory has not been used sufficiently as a foundation for understanding the communicative experience of oral history interviewing. This book is an effort to address that situation.

As an exercise in applied communication theory, this book is not prescriptive; it is analytic and descriptive. The explanation of the communicative dynamics that constitute oral interviewing and the description of cooperation and coherence achieved by interviewers and respondents are used to make the communicative process salient to readers. The objective is to direct critical thought toward the oral history interview process and, ultimately, toward its product, the oral text. As such, a caveat is in order. The analysis is based on American English discourse practices, linguistic constraints, and conversational and interview conventions. It is possible that specific conventions governing interview discourse vary among cultures. Hence I make no claims about generalizability beyond the data discussed here. The extent to which claims about interview discourse practices may be applied beyond North American English-language users is a question that should be determined empirically.

The book is comprised of five chapters. Chapter 1, "The Oral History Interview as an Interpretive Communicative Event," presents philosophical hermeneutics as a theoretical orientation toward communication in the oral history interview. The communicative features of the interview method are explained within this hermeneutical framework.

Having presented the theoretical presuppositions that guide my analyses, chapter 2, "Achieving Cooperation and Coherence in the Single Role of Information Elicitor," contains analyses of those interviews in which the interviewer's role is restricted to an elicitor of information. By that I refer to those occasions in which the interviewer chooses not to challenge the informant or her/his account of a lived-experience. Such interview records can be found frequently in archives.

My interest is in how cooperation and coherence are achieved during the creation of such an unchallenged record.

Chapter 3, "Achieving Cooperation and Coherence in the Dual Roles of Information Elicitor and Assessor," is a discussion of a different interview context—one in which the interviewer both elicits information from the respondent and evaluates that information *for the record*. As would be expected, this situation calls for additional strategies for achieving cooperative, coherent talk.

Chapter 4, entitled "Storytelling in Oral History as Collaborative Production," is an exploration of a prevalent feature of oral history interviews—storytelling. Because stories are told regardless of the interviewer role, I discuss the phenomenon in a separate chapter. I approach story production as a collaborative effort on the part of oral historians and their respondents. In so doing, I examine the interactive processes that constitute storytelling.

Building on the analyses reported in the foregoing discussion, chapter 5, "Communication-Related Issues for Oral Historians," links theory and practice by presenting current conceptions about human communication that are pertinent for understanding oral history interviewing. These presuppositions about the nature of human communication as practiced in oral history provide a foundation for understanding oral history interviewing as a complex communicative event.

The chapter also explores issues in oral history that are derived from an interpretive orientation toward communication. I use the term *interpretive orientation* to encompass diverse theoretical approaches to the study of human interpretive processes. Within the field of human communication such approaches are represented by the Chicago school of symbolic interaction, the University of Illinois program of constructivism, Alfred Schutz's phenomenological social theory, Aaron Cicourel's ethnomethodology, and the philosophical hermeneutics of Heidegger and Gadamer. The commonality here is that all of these approaches are grounded in the belief that in order to understand human existence one must deal with interpretation as central to that existence. As such, chapter 5 is concerned with issues that are raised whenever oral interviews are captured on audiotape and whenever they are translated into distinctive forms such as video and print. My intention in the final chapter is to shed some light on the problems of interpretation and editing with which oral historians are grappling.

Acknowledgments

Completion of this book would not have been possible without the financial support of the National Endowment for the Humanities Summer Stipend Program, the University of Alabama Research Grants Committee, and the Research and Service Committee of the College of Communication at the University of Alabama. Likewise, the John F. Kennedy Library, the New Jersey Historical Commission, and the University of Alabama Libraries were generous in their assistance. The University of Alabama Press also deserves my gratitude for selecting manuscript reviewers who provided helpful suggestions and for facilitating the book's completion.

In the same vein, I am grateful to the Department of Speech Communication at the University of Alabama for both the moral and secretarial support made available to me through the book's development. Invaluable research assistance was provided by William Purcell, Nancy Jackson, Maurice Stuckey, Joe Gow, Neal Flum, Laura Cullinane, and Jon Smekrud. To all of you, thank you for your superior work and for your good humor. I am also grateful to Jesse Delia and to the Department of Speech Communication at the University of Illinois for providing early insights which led to the development of this book.

It is extremely difficult to thank the people who are inextricably bound to a creative effort because so much of the credit (and none of the blame) for the work's development belongs to them. In my case, those people are Annabel D. Hagood, E. Culpepper Clark, and Anne Gabbard-Alley. Each of you served in so many roles: reader, teacher, friend, and editor. I am deeply indebted to you for your intellectual input, for your unswerving faith in me and my project, and for your lasting friendship.

Transcription Notation System

1. Simultaneous utterances are depicted by double left-handed brackets [[.
2. Overlapping utterances that do not start simultaneously are depicted by a single bracket. A single left-handed bracket [marks the point at which the overlap begins. A single right-handed bracket] marks the end of the overlap. When overlapping utterances are latched onto by a subsequent utterance, a single right-handed bracket and an equals sign]= are used.
3. Contiguous utterances are depicted by an equals sign =. There is no interval between adjacent utterances.
4. Intervals within the stream of talk are depicted in tenths of a second by a single parenthesis (0.0).
5. Characteristics of speech delivery:
   A co:lon depicts an extension of a sound of a syllable. Longer extensions are depicted by more co::lons.
   A period . depicts a falling tone.
   A comma , depicts continuing intonation.
   A question mark ? depicts a rising inflection.
   An exclamation point ! depicts an animated tone.
   A single dash – means halting or abrupt cutoff. Multiple dashes indicate a stammering quality of talk.
   Bold type means emphasis.

An hhh means audible aspirations.

An .hhh means audible inhalations.

6. Double parenthesis (( )) means vocalizations or other sounds occurring at the scene or characterizations of the talk or other details of the scene.

7. A single parenthesis when empty indicates no hearing could be achieved. A single parenthesis is also used to indicate doubt on the part of the transcriptionist.

8. .

.

. means elipsed turns at talk.

. . . means elipsed talk within a turn.

9. Statements enclosed within single brackets indicate speech acts and propositions. (Drawn from Schenkein 1978)

Elite Oral History
Discourse

1

The Oral History Interview as an Interpretive Communicative Event

(01) R: Okay, let me ((uh)) ask you about the relationships with other agencies then. ((uh)) To what extent were you directly or indirectly part of the National Security Council? I'm particularly interested in whether there was a special relationship there, of course, with Bill Bundy and Mac Bundy.

(02) E: ((uh uh)) Well, of course, you couldn't avoid a direct relationship between Bill Bundy and Mac Bundy.

(03) R: Right.

(04) E: But I don't know that this really affected the way things were handled. We worked very closely with State and had representatives from State in the Pentagon, ((uh)) for various meetings, although more often I was over at State.

R: [uh huh]

E: =In connection with these problems we got to know the ((uh)) AID people as well as the State Department people rather well because . . . always worked closely together ((uh)) the military assistance and the economic assistance groups. We tried to mesh them as closely as we could the ((uh)) objectives sometimes differed, country by country.

(05) R: In what way?

(06) E: Well ((uh)) I thought of that when I said it. Now I've got to come up with an example.[1]

I begin this chapter with this excerpt in order to illustrate my belief that oral history interviewing is most appropriately viewed as an interpretive communicative event. By that I mean the oral interview method involves the interview participants actively coping with the communicative performances of self and other. In this excerpt, the interviewee eloquently illustrates this performance by saying, "I thought of that when I said it. Now I've got to come up with an example." Throughout this book I will turn to oral history discourse as the primary object of scrutiny, thereby demonstrating how oral historians can add to their understanding of the oral interview method as an interpretive communicative process.

My purpose in this chapter is to lay the groundwork for subsequent discourse analyses by explaining the communicative features of the oral interview method when viewed within a hermeneutical or interpretive framework. The chapter contains an explanation of the nature of historical understanding vis-à-vis philosophical hermeneutics, an examination of the communicative experience of the oral history interview when viewed as a hermeneutical situation, a discussion of oral history discourse as rational action, and an explanation of the constraints that operate in oral history interviewing.

Philosophical Hermeneutics, Historical Understanding, and the Oral History Interview

Strictly speaking, philosophical hermeneutics refers to the science of interpretation.[2] The following discussion, however, is based on the "new hermeneutics," growing out of the works of philosophers such as Hans-Georg Gadamer, Martin Heidegger, and Paul Ricoeur.[3] Adoption of this paradigm as a basis for understanding oral history involves the acceptance of a nontraditional approach toward interpreting the meaning of historical phenomena.

The traditional approach, exemplified in the works of E. D. Hirsh,[4] views the "true" meaning of a work—such as a historical text—as residing within the intentions of the author of the text. The claim is that "while the *importance* of any work may vary with time and within different interpretive contexts, the one underlying meaning of the work does not change. The meaning of the text—which, on this account, is the author's willed meaning—is said to be self-identical, determinate, and reproducible (that is, sharable rather than private)."[5] To interpret the meaning of the text, therefore, requires that historians be "objective" and eliminate all prejudices associated with their present understanding of the phenomenon. The goal is to reorient oneself back in time to the context in which the text was originated. By so doing, the historian is able to "discover the true or intended meaning" of the phenomenon—what was meant by the author.

Philosophical hermeneutics rejects this traditional paradigm of historical understanding because of the "ontological primacy" it gives to human historicity: "the historicity of the historian's interpretation is one of the necessary pre-conditions of his hermeneutic understanding. . . . There is no neutral standpoint outside of history upon which the historian could found himself."[6]

Here, three presuppositions of hermeneutic theory are pertinent. First, "the oral historian must realize that the interpretation of any historic phenomenon is always performed within the universe of linguistic possibilities, and that these linguistic possibilities as performed mark out the historicality of human experience."[7] Human experience, hence human understanding, are temporally and culturally bound by the linguistic possibilities available to members of a given culture, for example, oral historians and respondents. The term *linguistic possibilities* refers to the diverse forms that language assumes in its diachronic development. It is through the linguistic possibilities that humans experience and understand their existence.

Second, "the interpretation of a historical phenomenon always is guided by the biases that an interpreter has at a specific moment in time. When such biases, as they induce meanings of a historical phenomenon, fail to provide direction toward what the phenomenon actually means for the interpreter's own culture, they must be reformulated."[8]

Third, "an act of interpretation must always be concerned directly with the historical phenomenon itself, e.g., not with an interviewee's intended meaning, but with what the intended meaning is about. Because any understanding of a historical phenomenon varies over time due to the linguistic possibilities that interpreters perform when signifying the phenomenon's supposed meaning, all interpretations of the phenomenon are to a certain extent subjective";[9] for as Gadamer reveals, "understanding is not so much a method by means of which the enquiring mind approaches some selected object and turns it into objective knowledge, as something of which a prior condition is its being situated within a process of tradition."[10]

From this viewpoint, the historicity of human experience precludes the possibility of the view of historical understanding put forth by traditionalists, where "truth" can be discovered by identifying the author's or the agent's intended meaning. On the contrary, historians/interpreters are constrained by their historicity in that "every putative re-cognition of a text or a pattern of behavior is really a new and different cognition of which the interpreter's own historicity is a constitutive part."[11] As Ebeling observes, the nature of interpretation is "to say the same thing in a different way and, precisely by virtue of saying it in a different way, to say the same thing. If by way of pure repetition, we were to say today the same thing that was said 2,000 years ago, we would only be imagining that we were saying the same thing, while actually we would be saying something quite different."[12] Hence, "a generation will not only understand itself differently from the way a past generation understood itself, it will also understand that past generation differently from the way the past generation understood itself."[13]

According to philosophical hermeneutics, then, the process of interpretation that occurs in oral history is manifested in the communicative performances of the interactants. The interpretative acts of thinking and speaking signify the meaning of the linguistic possibilities within the particular communication context. Historical understanding of data generated from an oral history interview must be predicated on an understanding of what occurs during the interview as the interactants negotiate the meanings of their lived-through experiences through their speech performances.[14] Grele concurs, noting that "the documents [oral historians] produce are artifacts of the time of their creation, not the period under discussion."[15] Moreover, those data must be regarded as the joint intellectual products of interviewer and interviewee.

The Communicative Experience of the Oral History Interview

As defined earlier, oral history is a conversation with a person whose life experience is regarded as memorable. This conversation, however, cannot be regarded as comparable to other documentary modes of inquiry. This is because the oral interview is a form of inquiry in which the evidence originates in the act of oral, face-to-face communication. The oral history interview is the joint intellectual product of a process wherein understanding is aided through speech and counterspeech. It is the intervention of the historian qua interviewer that serves as the impetus for the production of such historical data. The historian is the catalyst for as well as a participant in the creation of the historical record.

The most singular characteristic of an oral history, and by far its most significant for the historian as both creator and user, is its creation through the intervention of the historian. . . . An oral history, unlike an autobiography, and unlike oral traditions, would not exist without the active intervention of the historian. It is a document created as a result of the interests, questions, values, ambitions, ideas and drive of the historian. The story, the tale, the explanation, of course, exist without the historian, but the record and its particular form exist only through the active agency of the historian interviewer.[16]

Thus, contrary to Hans Jonas's claim that "historical understanding has only the one-sided speech of the past,"[17] oral history as an investigative form provides the entry point or wedge into historical understanding that, like present understanding, is aided by both speech and counterspeech. The result is "a different kind of text, based to be sure upon the stories we have been told but elaborated upon under our questioning."[18] The process by which that unique text is created is the communicative experience of the oral history interview.[19] In order to elucidate the features of this communicative process, certain presuppositions derived from an interpretive orientation toward human communication must be presented. The question to be answered is this: What does it mean to conceptualize the synchronic interview event as an open system? To characterize the oral history interview as an open system means that the elements of the face-to-face interchange are related in such a way that the system cannot be understood by analyzing its discrete elements alone. Rather, there is a complementary relationship between the whole and its parts wherein "The anticipated understanding of the whole is to be complemented and deepened by means of a better understanding of the parts; and yet, it is only within the light of the whole that the parts can play their clarifying roles."[20] So it is with understanding a communicative event as an open system. Such a characterization implies that the whole is greater than the sum of its parts, that the parts exist in an ongoing synergistic relationship, that the interactants engage in a process of reciprocal influence, and that their goals, be they shared or individualized, can be reached through a variety of paths that will be discovered while in the act of communicating. In other words, the synchronization of the speech performances by the actors calls all of these elements into play in light of the whole and vice versa.

In addition, the interview as an open system must be understood as developmental or evolutionary. There are two senses of development that are pertinent. The first pertains to the transactions that occur between interviewers and interviewees. Here the development or evolution simultaneously occurs within two message dimensions: (1) the content of the discourse, or what is said about the topic; and (2) the relationship dimension, or that which is expressed about how each individual is regarded by the other. This multidimensional process is conveyed simultaneously through verbal and nonverbal cues and continuously evolves during the course of an encounter. Indeed, just as one cannot walk in the same river twice, so the interactants cannot cover the same propositional and relational ground twice. Instead, they build on their experiences. In this way, all communicative experiences, including the oral history interview, are evolutionary or developmental in nature.

Because so much of the relational development in oral communication is conveyed nonverbally (e.g., voice tone or pitch, body language), an understanding of this developmental feature as it occurs in interviews must be predicated on the interviewer's deliberate attempt to capture that relational development and to convey same to subsequent users of the data. This can be accomplished through the use of audio/video recording, through note taking on the part of the interviewer, and through noting the nonverbal cues for the record. Such information can serve as a partial foundation for eventual judgments about the quality of the data as historical evidence.

The second sense of development or evolution that is pertinent to this discussion of the oral history interview pertains to the hermeneutical relationship between historian and respondent as they seek to probe the lived-through experience of the informant. That hermeneutical relationship is understood as a dialectical structure. The fundamental dialectic is between creativity and tradition wherein "the social reconstruction of reality is seen to involve an interplay of individual and socially constituted processes and contexts."[21] Even in the synchronic moment of communication, there is the dialectical relationship between tradition and creativity for both participants. In that instance, the tradition is the "happening" of the episode between self and other (the interlocutors); the creativity occurs as the interactants transcend the constraints of tradition. There is a "fusion of horizons" that, in turn, becomes the basis for the next episode of the encounter. The episodes of the interview, therefore, provide the opportunity for the interactants to develop, or to transform, or to "fuse" their interpretations; and by so doing, they create a historical tradition of the experience itself. This is because "understanding is circular and not linear, since understanding is necessarily situated, and as the situation changes, so does the understanding (a change in understanding bringing about a change in the situation)."[22]

Consequently, the historian as creator and user of oral history interview data should be sensitive to the systemic nature of face-to-face, oral communication. For example, as a participant in the communication process, the interviewer must try to be sensitive to the particular synergistic relationships that constitute each synchronic moment as well as to the underlying dialectical structure of the dialogue. One way to tap this complexity would be to conduct debriefing sessions with the interviewees in which the topic would be the lived-through experience of the interview. Here both historian and respondent would listen to or view the taped session in order to articulate their perceptions of what was happening between them. In addition, users of the data must try to preserve the complexity of the communicative event. Such a goal can be accomplished through the use of audio recordings in conjunction with the written transcriptions. In fact, there is no justification whatsoever for considering the written transcription to be equivalent to the interview process. Such action transforms the product into a phenomenon that is antithetical to the essence of oral history as an open, developmental system wherein historian and respondent jointly create a historical record.

The notion of joint creation stems from the view "that there is more to communicating than mere behavior exchange and the transmission of messages in some code."[23] In the synchronic interview event, there are two levels at which this joint intellectual effort, or joint construction of reality, takes place. The most basic level is the interaction situation itself. Generally, such explicit construction of reality would focus on the purpose of the interview, the time allotted for interaction, the use of recording equipment, legal concerns, and so on. Implicit in this construction process would be the situational identities of both parties, the interpersonal relationship between the two (e.g., the immediate social relations based on variables such as race, gender, and status), and the situational and cultural constraints applicable to the oral interview such as rules of turn-taking and topic selection. As Rommetveit explains, "We are . . . speaking on the premises of the listener, and listening on the premises of the speaker. And we are engaged in all these activities under conditions of variant, though most often institutionally taken-for-granted or personally familiar I-you coordinates of human interaction."[24] All of these elements will remain implicit, or taken for granted, until either party makes them the focus of the interaction. The second level of reality construction pertains to discourse about the interview topic. Through their communicative performances the interactants construct, coordinate, and negotiate their perceptions of the topic of conversation as well as their perceptions of the communicative performances that take place during the interview. Turning again to the excerpt that begins this chapter, certain expectations that govern the interaction situation itself are made explicit by the interviewee's commentary, "I thought of that when I said it, now I've got to come up with an example." In other words, the respondent anticipates that a particular type of answer will result in the need for further elaboration through an example. The interviewer confirms that expectation by asking for such a response. In addition, the discourse itself is topically oriented. Hence both parties engage in focused discussion until a new topic is introduced.

Communicative acts such as these combine to produce the joint intellectual performance that is the oral history interview. As illustrated above, the probable interpretations of statements and the likely implications of engaging in certain performance patterns can be located in the discourse itself, providing a vehicle for analyzing and understanding the oral interview method as a joint social construction process.[25] Furthermore, the social construction process that is manifested through the spoken word has a methodological advantage as contrasted with that of the written word. Whereas "no one could come to the aid of the written word if it falls victim to misunderstanding, intentional or unintentional,"[26] the spoken word can be illuminated through the interactional process itself. This illumination process is available to users as the oral (or video) text. Furthermore, these oral history data must be understood and utilized in ways that do justice to their emergent and jointly creative qualities. By so doing, oral historians would be moving toward understanding what Paul Thompson terms "the secret of [the] full potential" of the oral interview method—its "flexibility." For Thompson, flexibility means a "method based on a *combination* of exploration and questioning, within the context of a *dialogue* with the informant. It is a basic assumption of this dialogue that the researcher comes to learn the unexpected as well as the expected; and also that the overall framework within which information is given is determined not by the researcher, but by the informant's view of his or her own life."[27] Hence, remaining true to its creative, interactional essence the spoken word, unlike the written word, can come to the aid of historical understanding through the process of speech and counterspeech.

By now, to say that oral history communication is contextual seems to be stating the obvious. The importance of this idea, however, mitigates against taking it for granted. The synchronic elements of context, then, are those that constitute the communicative interaction as it occurs. These elements include the relationship of the social actors, their utterances and nonverbal cues as well as other extralinguistic factors such as time, location, and occasion. The meaning of any speech performance, therefore, is dependent upon the particular configuration of these contextual factors. The same utterance can be interpreted in more than one way depending upon the synchronic elements of context. For instance, the utterance, "Hi, how are you doing?" most likely will be interpreted as a ritualistic greeting requiring no more than a "Fine, how are you?" in the situation of two acquaintances passing one another in the hall at work. In the context of the Kentucky Derby, however, the same utterance most likely will be interpreted as a request for information about the other's "luck with the horses." An appropriate response, therefore, would be to recount one's record to the inquiring party. All social actors rely on their commonsense knowledge of exemplar situations to figure out the meanings of the discourse, as well as appropriate responses, as the discourse emerges through interaction in a particular setting.

The synchronic elements of context that play such an important role in meaning construction are another reason why the oral history interview must be understood as a communicative process—as "living speech," because, as Gadamer says, "The spoken word interprets itself to an astonishing degree, by the way of speaking, the tone of voice, the tempo etc., but also by the circumstances in which it is spoken."[28] To do otherwise is to misconstrue the oral interview, the result of which will be a distortion of the meaning construction process in this unique type of historical inquiry. Theoretically, then, the synchronic elements of context underlie and justify Henige's claim that "Failing informants themselves, it is inescapable that the tapes will be considered the historian's primary sources . . . only tapes provide such useful signals as pauses or other hesitations, variations in inflection, or interruptions and indications of dissent from bystanders." Hence, as sources transcripts "must always remain inferior to the tapes."[29]

Closely related to the contextual nature of communication is the notion of communication as a reason-based process. Currently, many communication scholars believe that a reason-based explanation of communication is more appropriate than previous laws-based explanations. Reason-based explanations of human communication assume that humans are active (rather than passive) agents who engage in purposive (rather than reactive) behavior based upon their understandings of the goal-action linkages in the social world; that is, the actors have reasons for pursuing particular courses of action. These reasons are grounded in their perceptions of means-end relationships in the social world, including their views of historical processes.

Not all situations, of course, are such that these means-end relationships are salient to the actors beforehand. In fact, there is reason to be believe that accounts of actions are frequently formulated after the fact. Nor will all situations demand reflective, self-aware actions that are one type of reason-based action. Undoubtedly, the routine, or scripted,[30] occurrences of everyday life do not demand such consciousness of situation, of intentions of self and other, or of means-end relationships in social action. In these situations, one's "implicit communication theory" serves well. It is the case, however, that many communicative events possess the contextual qualities that demand proactive strategies or lines of action. In these instances, it is likely that the actors will consciously see to it that their behaviors are constructed with respect to the goal-action linkages known to them. Two common contextual features that call on actors' attention to means-end relationships are novelty and personal risk, both of which are pertinent to oral history.

In terms of novelty, the oral history interview is a first for both parties, at least during the initial encounter. In addition, the emergent quality of the conversation perpetuates the newness of the experience. Finally, in some instances, the interviewer, and more often the respondent, participates in an oral history interview for the first time.

With regard to personal risk, the oral history interview is filled with features of risk for both parties. For example, historians/interviewers have their reputations and personal integrity on the line. To a certain extent, the historian/interviewer will be judged by peers on the basis of the data obtained and on the subsequent use of the data. The respondent, likewise, will experience personal risk in that one's account of the lived-through experience is for the record. The account is recorded and will be made available to interested third parties. Hence, one's personal identity—one's definition of self and of one's role or place in history—is on view. In these senses, then, the oral history interview is a paradigm of the reason-based communicative event. An understanding of the oral history interview as a hermeneutical situation, therefore, requires attention to its reason-based features.

In summary, the communication process of oral history interviewing can be characterized as an open system that is developmental, creative, contextual, and reason based. These ideas must be used in order to understand the synchronic relationship between historians and respondents as they enact their communicative performances that, in turn, enable the other relationships of the hermeneutical situation to come into being. Two of those relationships, between the historian and the historical event and between the respondent and the historical event, are explained in the next section.

The Diachronic Relationship Between the Interactants and the Historical Event

The relationships between the interactants and the historical event are diachronic in nature. As a researcher, the oral historian brings an informed perspective of the historical event. Even so, that perspective is, as Kockelmans would note, a reflection of the historicity of historical interpretation. The historian's viewpoint, then, is the product of the evolution of historical tradition that is itself "a succession of synchronic moments. These synchronic moments of understanding, interpreting, and giving meaning to the historical phenomenon are such that its meaning is conveyed to the present."[31]

Although the respondent/historical event relationship is also diachronic in nature, respondents bring their own perceptions of events formed from actual experience—the memory of lived-through experience. "Since any lived experience can acquire meaning only to the extent that it is 'reflected upon' after it occurs, the interviewee's knowledge of the event develops diachronically."[32] The meaning of the lived experience depends upon the "temporal distance" of the interviewee. "Temporal distance is not a distance to be travelled through, but a living continuity of elements which as links in a chain constitute the tradition which, taken as a whole, functions as the light in which everything with which we are confronted (i.e., which is now being handed down to us) can appear as that which it really is."[33] Storytelling, as discussed by Bertaux, is illustrative of the phenomenon of temporal distance: "stories about the past are told from the present, from a situation which may have changed over the years and defines a new relationship to the past. It is *this relationship* which underlies the whole story. . . . Telling a story about the past is a way of expressing indirectly a meaning about the present."[34]

Finally, the interdependent relationship among interviewer, interviewee, and the historical event reflects the holistic and complex nature of the oral history interview as a hermeneutical situation. The hermeneutical situation is both synchronic and diachronic and as such directs attention to the jointly creative process wherein the meaning of a historical event at a particular moment in time is produced. This production of meaning can be conceptualized as a process of mediation between the dialectical relations that inhere in the hermeneutical situation: between the old and the new, between tradition and creativity, between the individual and the social, between self and other, between the interlocutor and the "imagined audience"—those persons who might have access to the tapes and transcriptions now or in the future—between the fleeting moment of "living speech" and the "fixed inscription" of the oral text.

The creative, emergent process of interpretive interaction is worked out not only within a set of socio-historically inherited constraints (sociolinguistic rules, definitions of prototypical situations and contexts, etc.) but also within a set of situationally emergent constraints. Individuals must create strategies which actualize their intentions, but which do so within the constraints imposed by the contextually-constituted definitions given to situation, self, other relationships, and the focus of interaction. They must introduce their projects into the interactional agenda, securing focused attentions for their concerns. The strategies generated thus must not only actualize their intentions, but also must be appropriate within the constantly emerging definition given to reality in interaction.[35]

Such is the complexity of the hermeneutical situation as it shows itself in the communicative experience of oral history.

To summarize to this point, human communication is characterized as a reason-based process through which intersubjective reality is constructed. Specifically, human communication is depicted as a process of reciprocally imputing and negotiating intentions and meaning, the product being intersubjectively established knowledge. As a reason-based process, emphasis is placed on the goal-directed nature of communication. Likewise, oral history interviewing as a form of human communication is explained as goal-directed interaction through which historian and respondent jointly create a historical record in the form of an oral text. In fact, I have suggested that the hermeneutical situation of oral history interviewing is a paradigm of a reason-based event. In the following section, the implications of viewing oral history conversation as reason-based communication (or rational action) are considered as a way of providing background for the discussion of the discourse analytic method used in this investigation.

Oral History Discourse as Rational Action

Central to an actional view of human behavior is the belief that humans are capable of and, in fact, do engage in goal-directed activity. As such, courses of action can be deliberately selected based on an agent's understanding of the means-end relationships that are present in that agent's commonsense world. Furthermore, goal-directed activity implies that the course of action chosen will be, in the actor's judgment, the best way to achieve the goal under the present circumstances. In other words, people have reasons for acting as they do. Schutz terms such activity as "rational action on the common-sense level."[36]

"[R]ational action" on the common-sense level is always action within an unquestioned and undetermined frame of constructs of typicalities of the setting, the motives, the means and ends, the courses of action and personalities involved and taken for granted. They are, however, not merely taken for granted by the actor but also supposed as being taken for granted by the fellow-man. From this frame of constructs, forming their undetermined horizon, merely particular sets of elements stand out which are clearly and distinctly determinable. To these elements refers the common-sense concept of rationality.[37]

Rational action on the commonsense level, then, is goal-directed activity based on one's best understanding of the means-end relationships operable within a given situation. As such, the choice of courses of action is always context dependent and probable in outcome. This means that the value of the information taken into account can change relative to the situation, but the process of assessing that information in terms of means-end relationships remains constant.

Although many scholars[38] have written at length about the

nature of rational action and about the methods most appropriate for explaining such action, most seem to agree on two points: that the accomplishment of rational action involves some sort of imaginative rehearsal of contingent means-end connections and their consequences within the context of operable constraints on those contingencies; and that culturally bounded rules of conduct are used by the actors as a framework for making those judgments. For example, "The archetypal or paradigm process by which social action is generated involves the imaginative preplaying [what Schutz calls "fantasying"] of an episode in the course of which various possible patterns are envisaged and checked for their effects and their social propriety, and in the course of which they are related to rules or rule-surrogates such as already established paradigms."[39] This means that people "orient their actions on certain standards which are socially approved as rules of conduct by the in-group to which they belong."[40]

My contention is that many communicative behaviors, like many forms of human behavior, consist of rational action on the commonsense level. For example, individuals such as the interviewee in the earlier excerpt monitor and attempt to control their communicative performances (expecting reciprocity from others). The monitoring process is grounded in the "systematic social expectations of others" and in "the accepted code of the primary actors, that is . . . the rules."[41] Moreover, communicative situations that are novel or that carry with them personal risk or notoriety for the interactants require communicative performances based on a consciousness of purpose inherent within rational action. It follows, therefore, that the interpretive communicative event of the oral history interview, which exhibits all of the above features, can be characterized as paradigmatic of communication as rational action. By definition, then, the oral history interview as a reason-based or rational communicative event is one in which the actors engage in communicative performances based on perceived goal-action relationships and in which the actors, through reflexive awareness, actively monitor and assess the communicative interaction that occurs.

The monitoring occurs at two levels that parallel the ways that discourse functions to affect meaning. These are the propositional level—locution, or what is said—and the performative level—language as action. The levels of discourse show themselves, for example, in the negotiation and coordination of probable interpretations of the historical event itself as well as in the negotiation and coordination of the interpersonal coordinates of the face-to-face situation, (e.g., situational identities, the interpersonal relationship, etc.). In terms of propositional content, the production and management of discourse is judged according to the criterion of coherence; that is, interlocutors are expected to show local and global relatedness of their dialogue at the propositional level. With respect to the performative level, or language as action, the monitoring of coherence pertains to two levels of speech actions: (1) illocution—what is done in the act of saying; and (2) perlocution—what is done by the saying (the effect produced by the illocution).[42] In addition, the relationship between the propositional and the performative levels is monitored. In short, coherence of the communicative interaction is a product of both propositional and pragmatic (functional) coherence. Given the above, certain observations about the contextual constraints on the communicative performances occurring in the hermeneutical situation of the oral history interview are necessary.[43]

The Interview Situation

Topical constraints

The subject matter of the interview serves as a constraint on the dialogue that occurs during the interview. Although the interviewer possesses more legitimate control of the topic selection and management, the interviewee's legitimacy derives from having lived through the experience. Moreover, the interviewee has the opportunity to exert situational control through the kinds of answers provided to the questions and through the speech actions that are performed during the course of the exchange. In so doing, certain topics can become the focus of extended turn expansions, whereas other topics can remain unrevealed. Moreover, topics are constrained by the goals, the structure, and procedures of the oral interview itself.

Goal-related constraints

The overriding goal in oral history, of course, is to obtain testimony about a memorable, lived-through experience. Additionally, the oral historian's goals could be to verify factual data, to confirm a particular interpretation of an account, to pursue a specific agenda of issues, or to test hypotheses. The informant, on the other hand, may be seeking to establish a particular image for himself or herself with regard to the historical event in question, or the informant may be seeking to protect an established public image. Whatever the particular scenario might be, both parties approach the interview with multiple goals to accomplish during the course of the interview. Certain of these goals are made explicit; others remain implicit.

Procedural constraints

Recognizing that oral interviews impose procedural constraints on the interactants, certain typicalities relevant to conducting the interview are operative and nonnegotiable. For example, an interview by definition occurs by virtue of taking turns at talking, wherein the question/answer adjacency pair in a preallocated turn-taking system is the exemplar. In light of this system, certain role behaviors (i.e., interviewer as interrogator and interviewee as respondent) suggest that control of the interaction relative to issues such as introduction and management of topics is the legitimate domain of the interviewer. The respondent, on the other hand, acquires situational control of such procedural matters only through conversational strategies enacted during the course of the interview. Moreover, such conversational moves must be enacted in relation to certain metarules or conversational maxims that govern interview conduct. Of particular relevance here is the principle of cooperativity, be cooperative with your conversational partner[44]—that is, show your cooperativity by being relevant, by saying neither too little nor too much, and by saying things that are worthwhile and true.

Finally, such conversational activity presupposes that what a speaker means in an utterance is inextricably linked to what action that speaker is performing by virtue of making the utterance and that, in fact, conversationalists routinely make both propositional and illocutionary points.[45] Selection and enactment of propositions and illocutions within interview episodes result, in part, from each actor's consideration of the procedural constraints operating within the situation.

Structural constraints

Unlike casual conversation or other types of oral interviews in which only two parties are involved in the interaction, the oral history interview is constrained by an additional component, the imagined audience. Clearly, this third party to the interview is salient to both the oral historian and the respondent. In fact, the presence of the imagined audience is emphasized by the presence of recording equipment and by preinterview arrangements about copyright, release forms, and storage of materials. The salience of this component is often made clear by direct references during the interview to the record or to the recording equipment by oral historians and their respondents.

Finally, there is the dialectical structure inherent in the hermeneutical situation itself. The ideal type of the communicative experience of oral history interviewing is hermeneutical conversation, a dialectical process of communicative interaction that involves the articulation of conflicting perspectives of a historical phenomenon[46] and that is congruent with Grele's conception of the role of the oral historian as a cocreator of the historical record whose purpose is to transform individual stories into cultural narratives.[47]

Michael Hyde's structural model[48] is a portrayal of oral history conversation and of its potential for achieving a special form of dialectical interpretation through oral communication (see figure 1). Hermeneutical conversation is depicted as a

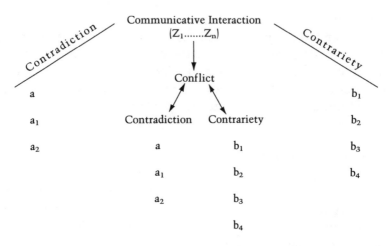

Figure 1. Hyde's Structural Model

structural layer within and a reflection of the fundamental dialectic that is interpretation.

In the model, *communicative interaction* is the face-to-face interaction between interviewer and interviewee. *Conflict* refers to the inherent conflicting perspectives, or different conceptions of the past, that the interlocutors bring to the discussion of the historical event. Each interactant, by virtue of his or her own life experience and relationship to the event in question (Z), will bring different perspectives to the face-to-face interaction. This is inevitable due to the nature of experience: each person brings his or her own historicity. Moreover, this historicity is constituted of "the taken-for-granted (*das Fraglos-gegeben*)." The taken-for-granted, Schutz explains, "is always that particular level of experience which presents itself as not in need of further analysis."[49] However, "a change of attention can transform something that is taken for granted into something problematical."[50] Moreover, "since the interviewee's memory . . . becomes the taken-for-granted assumptions directing the interviewee's discourse about the historical phenomenon, the goal of the oral historian is to make problematic the taken-for-granted assumptions of the interviewee—to confront his or her memory of lived-through experience."[51] For example, the oral historian, through questioning, directs a "reflective glance of attention" to the taken-for-grantedness of the respondent's recollection, thereby transforming the "given" into the "problematical."

Conflict, therefore, refers to the implicit tension that underlies the worldviews of the interactants as members of society. The interview situation provides the opportunity for the taken-for-granted assumptions that constitute those worldviews to be articulated and made problematical. The interview is where the implicit tension becomes explicit; that is, it emerges and evolves. It is this tension that Hyde calls conflict.[52] The emergence of this conflict is the point at which the *potential* of oral history conversation to become dialectical is realized.

Precisely how the conflict is transformed depends upon how the conflict is managed by the interactants; that is, how the *questioning* mediates the reflective glance of attention, turning the given into the problematical. As the model suggests, one possible transformation is *contradiction*, in which "each interactant affirms her/his own perception of the historical event which, in turn, results in disagreement."[53] For example, a respondent may "remember" his or her role in the event as being more active than the historian's perception would suggest. If their disagreement is not resolved, then the disagreement becomes reified as contradiction.

If, on the other hand, the interactants identify their differing perspectives, suspend their own perspectives, and at the same time acknowledge the potential validity of the other's meaning, then *contrariety* emerges. The emergence of contrariety enables hermeneutical conversation to be actualized. For Gadamer,

To conduct a [hermeneutical] conversation means to allow oneself to be conducted by the object to which the partners in the conversation are directed. It requires that one does not try to outargue the other person, but that one really considers the weight of the other's opinion. Hence, it is an art of testing. But the art of testing is the art of questioning. For we have seen that to question means to lay open, to place in the open. As against the solidity of opinions, questioning makes the object and all its possibilities fluid. . . . Dialectic consists not in trying to discover the weakness of what is said, but in bringing out its real strength. It is not the art of arguing that is able to make a strong case out of a weak one, but the art of thinking that is able to strengthen what is said by referring to the object.[54]

Kockelmans further explains the "liberating" function of dialectical interaction:

Everyone knows how difficult it is to give up a prejudice and to substitute a new conviction in its place. The reason for this is that the new conviction can never be presented as the eternal truth. And what is more, the new conviction can never be specified adequately except in connection with the original prejudice whose part it now plays. It is by dialectic opposition that convictions become evaluated. Thus, we are led here to a new element, namely *the dialectic between the old and new.* The original, implicit prejudice which was not yet understood as a prejudice, functioned within the overall conception concerning a set of phenomena. My new conviction is not in harmony with the original overall conception. Adopting a new conviction means to give up part of my original overall understanding of those phenomenon. Thus, a dialectic process begins to take place between what is mine but appears to be inauthentic, and what is authentic but is not yet mine. Our interrogation which is the universal mediator of this dialectic will never reach a point where it becomes impossible to replace an implicit prejudice by a new conception which is still alien to me but which I shall have to make mine if I am really willing to comprehend the relevant set of phenomena.[55]

Whenever hermeneutical conversation is actualized four possible transformations of new meaning may emerge (see figure 1). Elsewhere I have termed these transformations *corrected meaning* and *constructed meaning.*[56] Corrected meaning (b_1 and b_2) refers to instances in which one of the person's meaning is disaffirmed, and that person acquires a new meaning of the lived-through experience. For example, a researcher's extensive knowledge of demographic data concerning an event often serves a corrective function during the actual interview. In a similar vein, the respondent, due to actual participation in the event, can modify the researcher's second-hand knowledge.

For those interested in the creative potential of dialectic, the transformations termed *constructed meaning* (b_3 and b_4) hold the most exciting possibilities. Here the element of joint discovery characterizes the situation. "Here both parties are able through their conversation to evolve new understandings of an event either by affirming or disaffirming their prior conceptions. In this way, both parties share in the creation of *new* meaning—meaning which emerges out of mutual affirmation or disaffirmation of prior understandings of the historical event."[57]

The actual selection and enactment of conversational routines at the propositional level and at the illocutionary level within episodes are the result of each actor's consideration of the elements discussed above as well as each actor's reciprocal adaption to the interaction itself. Hence the production of *discourse as ideas* and *discourse as action* is displayed by the talk that evolves over the course of the interview. It is this display of talk that is the focus of discourse analysis.

Summary

This chapter lays the foundation for viewing the oral history interview as an interpretive communicative event. Groundwork is laid for discourse analysis by discussing the nature of historical understanding demanded by the "new philosophical hermeneutics." The synchronic and diachronic communicative features of an oral history interview when conceptualized from an interpretive orientation and the theory of philosophical hermeneutics have been explained. In particular, implications relative to viewing the oral text as the product of collaborative rational action by historian and respondent have been presented. Chapter 2 covers background information for the analysis of elite oral history discourse. Specifically, there is discussion of the achievement of conversational cooperation and coherence whenever oral historians restrict the interviewer's role to that of information elicitor.

2

Achieving Cooperation
and Coherence
in the Single Role of
Information Elicitor

(01) R: If we can go back now =
(02) E: [Yeah].
(03) R: = to the governor's conference. How effective was the conference in generating support for the legislation?
(04) E: I think it was very effective because afterwards many of
the congressmen and particularly the senators would say,
"Oh, yes, the governor spoke to me about that." Now the
Republican governors, of course, ((uh)) didn't do their
homework ((uh)) they urged to vote against it on party lines.
Mr. Halleck was hard nosed on party lines. He was not a
governor, but he was a Republican whip in Congress.[1]

Having laid the theoretical groundwork for viewing the oral
history interview as an interpretive communicative event, the
purpose of this chapter is twofold: (1) to present a framework
for analyzing the discourse that is performed in the hermeneutical situation of oral history interviewing; and (2) to describe the accomplishment of cooperation and coherence in
interview situations in which the interviewer's role is restricted to eliciting (as contrasted with assessing) information.[2] My approach, based primarily on the ideas of scholars
in philosophy, linguistics, sociolinguistics, psychology, and
communication,[3] is discourse analysis. Although discourse

analysis is not the only framework applicable to communicative events such as the oral history interview, the subject area can provide insights into the interpretive work as displayed by the interactants, the idea being that such a description constitutes a partial account of how meaning construction occurs in elite oral history.

The importance of accounting for how practitioners of oral history achieve cooperation and coherence is found in the relationship between the process of oral interviewing and its product(s). The discourse itself displays the unfolding thought processes. Rather than showing the last thing one thinks as in writing, conversation shows the first, second, third, etc., transformations of thought as the interaction evolves. Conversations such as the one that opens this chapter display the interactive nature of the process by which both parties influence the outcome. In other words, the dialogue between the participants displays the "question-and-answer complex" that underlies the explication of the historical event.[4] Moreover, the meanings of the questions and answers are contextually grounded and negotiated by the interlocutors. Thus attention to the performance context of the oral interview is necessary for understanding the nature of the historical products generated through that communicative process.

Toward that end, this chapter is divided into three sections: (1) a discussion of discourse analysis as a subject area that can inform an examination of oral history discourse production as rational action; (2) presentation of the methodological assumptions of this study; and (3) a descriptive analysis of the principles of conversational production used for achieving cooperation and coherence (propositional and pragmatic) in elite oral history interviews in which the interviewer's role is restricted to eliciting information from the respondent.

Discourse Analysis

Discourse analysis is a generic term referring to the study of language in use. Michael Stubbs, a noted sociolinguist, says that discourse analysis "attempts to study the organization of language above the sentence or above the clause, and therefore to study larger linguistic units, such as conversational exchanges or written texts. . . . It follows that discourse analysis is also concerned with language in use in social contexts, and in particular with interaction or dialogue between speakers."[5] A concern for language in use, of course, is not new. There exists a long, distinguished tradition in discourse analysis that transcends disciplinary boundaries. Notable authorities in the area include Gumperz and Hymes in anthropology, specifically ethnography; Goffman in sociology; Sacks and Schegloff in ethnomethodology; Austin, Searle, and Grice in philosophy; Labov and Fanshel in sociolinguistics; Jacobs, Jackson, and Nofsinger in communication; and Bach and Harnish in linguistics.[6] All of these scholars share a common interest: accounting for the accomplishment of conversation in everyday life. The goal is to explain how people accomplish the joint activity of conversing, regardless of the situation. As Stubbs puts it, "People are quite able to distinguish between a random list of sentences and a coherent text, and it is the principles which underlie this recognition of coherence which are the topic of study for discourse analysts."[7] "Whereas lingusitics studies language, discourse analysis can study the actual mechanisms by which communication, understanding, and interaction are maintained."[8] The analysis is accomplished by investigating how speakers display their understanding of each other's conversational work. The data, in other words, are generated by the conversationalists themselves, preferably in naturally occurring situations.[9]

A subject area as diverse as discourse analysis is inevitably comprised of a variety of research-related topics (e.g., turn-taking, repairs, coherence) and offers several approaches for conducting the analytical inquiries (e.g., sequencing rules, the move system, the rational model).[10] My interest in elite oral history discourse focuses on cooperation and coherence and is informed by research on both propositional and pragmatic (functional) coherence. What follows is an overview of pertinent substantive claims about conversational cooperation and coherence.

Just as social behavior is explained from the actional perspective in terms of rules, so conversational activity is grounded in rules-based explanations.[11] As such, rules "are probably best conceived as propositions that model, at varying levels of awareness, our understandings of the situated evaluation of social behavior, and the ways in which social interaction should be constituted and carried out."[12]

Most scholars agree that rules function as a basis for prediction, interpretation, and evaluation of social behavior. In the case of communicative behavior, for example, we expect that a conversation will end with a sequence of exchanges that brings closure to the encounter (e.g., summary, talk of next encounter) rather than ending abruptly with silence and immediate departure of one or both conversational partners. In fact, such anticipations are such a taken-for-granted feature of social interaction that they become obvious only upon violation of the convention.

In addition, rules provide the grounds for interpretation of communicative behavior. Interpretive rules, therefore, are statements that set forth the conditions that must be present in order for an utterance to "count as" a particular kind of proposition or a special type of speech act. The utterance "Do you have the time?" is illustrative. If interpreted literally, the question is asked in a yes-no form that could be answered as "Yes, I do." Such an answer, however, would be in violation of the interpretive rule of requests. Hence when one is asked the question "Do you have the time?" the question counts as a request to be told the time. Native speakers, of course, do not find communication based on such taken-for-granted interpretive rules at all problematic. In fact, expectations about appropriate communicative behaviors are based on such notions. Nonnative speakers, on the other hand, find such exchanges problematic until they discover the "unwritten interpretive rules" of the culture. The point is that interpretive rules provide a foundation for the negotiation of meaning in symbolic interaction.

Finally, rules serve as the measuring rods for the evaluation of behavior—as the basis for the critique of communicative behavior. Generally, conformity to the rules merits no special attention or praise. Failure to follow the rules, however, usually provokes attention, criticism, and sometimes negative sanction. For example, dressing properly for an employment interview warrants no special plaudits from the potential employer. Inappropriate attire, on the other hand, can serve as grounds for dismissal of the candidate as a potential employee. Similarly, proper use of grammar, of propositional content, and of performatives is expected from competent communicators. Communication competence, therefore, demands a knowledge of the rules that underlie communicative performances across a variety of situations.

In summary, rules are models of our understandings of how social behavior should be carried out. Communication rules provide similar understandings with regard to the performance and interpretation of symbolic interaction. Rules provide the foundation for the production, management, interpretation, and evaluation of communicative performance.

There is an additional level of knowledge believed to underlie communicative performance. This knowledge pertains to the grounds by which individuals come to understand how to apply particular rules to particular situations. There are several labels for this body of knowledge about conversational activity: metarules, principles, and maxims. Grice's cooperative principle, with its corollary maxims of "quantity," "relevance," and "manner," is a metarule believed to underlie virtually all communicative behavior:

Our talk exchanges do not normally consist of a succession of disconnected remarks, and would not be rational if they did. They are characteristically, to some degree at least, cooperative efforts; and each participant recognizes in them, to some extent, a common purpose or set of purposes, or at least a mutually accepted direction. This purpose or direction may be fixed from the start (e.g., by an initial proposal of a question for discussion), or it may evolve during the exchanges; it may be fairly definite, or it may be so indefinite as to leave very considerable latitude to the participants (as in a casual conversation). But at each stage, SOME possible conversational moves would be excluded as conversationally unsuitable. We might then formulate a rough general principle which participants will be expected (ceteris paribus) to observe, namely: Make your conversational contribution such as is required, at the stage at which it occurs, by the accepted purposes or direction of the talk exchange in which you are engaged. One might label this the COOPERATIVE PRINCIPLE.[13]

Furthermore, Grice proposes that if the cooperative principle is violated (e.g., by saying too much or too little, by making irrelevant comments, by being ambiguous or disorganized, by making unsupported claims), then the situation invites conversational implicature, "broadly construed, the engagement of a set of interpretive procedures designed to figure out just what the speaker is up to."[14] Suppose, for example, that an interviewer asks, "Where were you when you first met John F. Kennedy?" and the respondent answers, "My favorite story about Kennedy was told to me by his mother." There is no apparent connection between the question and the answer. In order to interpret the answer, one must assume that the answer violated the relevance maxim. Yet assuming that the respondent is trying to be cooperative, we also assume that the topic of where the person met Kennedy is off bounds and that the respondent is not inclined to pursue that topic. This interpretive procedure is called conversational implicature.

To summarize to this point, conversation is believed to be governed by rules about the appropriateness of utterances and actions in context.[15] The force of rules, because rule-governed behavior presupposes rational action based on choice, derives from their evaluative use by communicators. Individuals are expected to demonstrate their in-group membership as well as their communicative competence by applying the appropriate rules in context. In addition, rules function to predict, to interpret, and to evaluate communicative performances. The meaning of an utterance (hence the meaning of sequences of utterances or episodes) is thought to emerge from the connections between what the speaker means, what the utterance means, what the speaker intends, what the hearer understands, and what the rules governing the communicative performance are. In this sense, conversation, which is always grounded contextually, involves making statements (locutions), performing actions (illocutions), and achieving effects (perlocutions) based on the actions.

Methodological Assumptions

Throughout this book the oral history interview is defined as a conversation with a person whose life experience is deemed memorable. The data for analysis, selected for their conformity to this definition, are audiotapes and transcripts of fifty-four interviews (approximately 160 hours) conducted by oral historians. These data were obtained from the archives of the New Jersey Historical Commission, the John F. Kennedy Library, and the University of Alabama.

The method used to formulate the description of coherence in elite oral history discourse is a variation of analytic induction. "Analytic induction proposes the progressive formulation and testing of hypothesis through the observational process. As negative cases appear, they are made to fit the emergent hypothesis. If they cannot be explained, a revision of the hypothesis is demanded."[16] Hence analytic induction is a method used to achieve a comprehensive and exhaustive description of the phenomenon under investigation. In this instance, the phenomenon is elite oral history discourse that is produced during naturally occurring interviews by oral historians with elite informants. As defined earlier, elite informants are those persons who develop accounts of their involvement in controlling society as contrasted with nonelites who provide accounts of their lack of control.

In this investigation, the method of analytic induction is used within the conceptual framework of philosophical hermeneutics and discourse analysis. Specifically, Hyde's structural model of oral history interview conversation and principles of conversational coherence developed by discourse analysts are used as conceptual guides for the descriptive analyses.

When viewed from the perspective of discourse analysis, the oral history interview is a rule-governed, formal interrogation. As such, interviewing is a collaborative production organized by conventions of language use wherein two cooperative speakers jointly create the conventional interaction patterns within the context of topical, goal-related, procedural, and structural constraints discussed in chapter 1.

Propositional Coherence

Conversational coherence refers to the relatedness of utterances within a discourse context. Conversational coherence is a product of both propositional coherence and pragmatic coherence. In an interview, each utterance simultaneously serves as a proposition and functions as a speech act or illocution. Turns 03 and 04 from the opening excerpt serve as illustration:

> (03) R: = to the governor's conference. How effective was the conference in generating support for the legislation?
>
> (04) E: I think it was very effective because afterwards many of the congressmen and particularly the senators would say, "Oh yes, the governor spoke to me about that." Now the Republican governors, of course, ((uh)) didn't do their homework or ((uh)) they urged to vote against it on party lines. Mr. Halleck was hard nosed on party lines. He was not a governor, but he was a Republican whip in Congress.

Here turn 03 functions both as a proposition that introduces a topic—the relationship between the governor's conference and legislative support—and as an illocution—a request for information about the topic. In turn 04, the interviewee grants the request for information, the grant serving as the illocutionary act, and the propositional element of the turn is provided by the direct response to the main theme—legislative support generated by the governor's conference. Note also that a negotiation process is occurring relative to the topic because the interviewee takes the opportunity to expand the topic somewhat by introducing related but not equivalent themes: the role of the Republican governors and of the Republican whip, Mr. Halleck.

Just as this example suggests, the meaning and overall coherence of the interview discourse emerge as both propositional and pragmatic coherence are achieved. However, in order to emphasize certain points of analysis, I will treat propositional and pragmatic coherence separately in the following discussion.

Propositional coherence refers to the ways in which the utterances are about the same topic or theme. Not only must the turns at conversation fit together on a next-turn basis, but they must also fit in with the propositions or themes of the conversation in general—what the conversation is about. As McLaughlin observes, "coherence derives from an over-arching proposition, in light of which successive utterances are interpreted and constructed."[17] Likewise, propositional coherence in an interview conversation is dependent upon the local management of discourse as the interview evolves. Furthermore, it is assumed that the principle of cooperativity underlies the management of interview conversation. The conversation is conducted within the implicit framework of rules and devices for achieving cooperation. Implications about cooperativity in conversation can be gleaned from this foundation, suggesting that we expect people to "avoid tangential talk," "be relevant," and "respond directly to [a] partner's topic."[18]

In addition, conversationalists commonly use topic or propositional management devices during the course of routine conversation. Such devices are used to achieve subgoals such as topic shift, topic insertion, topic avoidance, and storytelling while maintaining the overriding goals of coherence and cooperativity. Similarly, oral historians and respondents (hereafter referred to as R and E) must accomplish subgoals of topic management while achieving coherence and cooperativity during the interview. The significance of understanding how cooperativity and coherence are achieved in elite oral history is suggested by Paul Thompson's discussion of the public personality as informant: "Such people ... may have such a strong idea of their own story, and what matters in it, that all they can offer is stereotyped recollections. They often also, in the course of long careers in public life, will have developed a protective shell by which they ward off troublesome questions and while seeming to say something worthwhile in fact give away as little as possible. . . . It is this defensive veil that the interviewer must penetrate."[19]

This and other aspects of interview talk are the concern of the following analysis. The data are audiotapes and transcripts of interviews where R's single role is neutral elicitor of information. As indicated earlier, the imagined audience is a significant structural constraint within the oral history interview situation. This unspecified third party can take many forms, such as R's colleagues, E's peers, future historians, and interested citizens. In essence, neither R nor E has control over the potential audiences to an interview. R, on the other hand, can control his or her relationship to E and to the interview record, thereby controlling indirectly his or her relationship to the imagined audience. A strategy used frequently by oral historians is to enact a role of neutral elicitor of information. This is where the interviewer elects to serve only as a catalyst for obtaining information about a lived-through experience. As such, the interviewer avoids offering assessments of the respondent's answers, thereby maintaining neutrality with regard to the interview record and the interviewee. One consequence of this limited interviewer role is the production of what appears to be planned accounts or story lines within the general context of the interview.[20] In other words, the respondent's answers, devoid of assessments by the interviewer, often take on the character of rehearsed or stereotypical recollection. Furthermore, any evaluation of the interview record is left to the imagined audience. Even so, the interaction itself is locally managed and must display coherence and cooperation, and the interviewer and respondent are obligated to achieve the overarching goal of discussing the informant's lived-through experience. How are these multiple goals achieved?

Topic management

Certain characteristics of elite oral history interview talk are pertinent to topic management, hence propositional coherence: (1) R's role as interrogator legitimizes overall topic control by R; (2) any utterance by R and E may be heard as containing or implying historically relevant (lived-through experience) topics on which R or E may comment; (3) topic talk is retroactive and locally managed. An implicit topic in a prior turn can become the explicit topic of a next turn; (4) the explicit topic can become an extended topic depending upon R's third-turn response; (5) although the adjacency pair (question-answer) is the fundamental structural unit of an interview, the three unit question-answer-response is the necessary structure for extended topic management, hence for eliciting information about a lived-through experience; and (6) as a neutral elicitor of information, R's possible third-turn responses are limited.

There is a striking parallel between topic management devices used in news interviews and in oral history interviews where R enacts the neutral role described earlier. In particular, three topic management devices—prompt, cooperative recycle, and inferentially elaborative probe—are pertinent to oral history.[21]

Interviewers are obligated to attempt to advance a report as well as to indicate a desired direction for the subsequent report. The prompt is a device used to achieve such formulations. The prompt is "some minor inference based on prior statements," and it is "used as a means to prompt interviewees to reconfirm and elaborate their prior remarks."[22] Two uses of prompts are displayed in the following excerpt from an interview.

In the preceding section of the interview, a former member of the Kennedy administration is discussing mental health legislation.[23]

(01) R: Did you have any discussions with President Kennedy about organizing the conference or the effects of the conference?

(02) E: No. That was all with Mike Feldman. But apparently the President was pleased. A lot of restraints that I just barely noticed then were taken off.

(03) R: Restraints? [Prompt/Request for Clarification]

(04) E: Restraints, yes. Prior to that time I had to report to Mike Feldman if I talked to a governor or a congressman, but after this ((uh)) Mike said, "Oh well, you've met most of them, and you got along well with their people." So ((uh)) apparently any suspicion that I might be a hot potato because I was a Republican and I might mess up ((laugh)) politics ((laugh)) was allayed.

(05) R: There was this suspicion? [Prompt/Request for Confirmation]

(06) E: Oh, I imagine. Well, wouldn't you if you took into your fold a man of the opposite party? You might suspect that

there would be a little dragging of heels occasionally on things, but this was a nonpartisan thing. I considered it a professional problem so that politics didn't enter into it, and I was only anxious to get it passed.

In turn 03, for example, R selects one word—"restraints"— introduced by E to focus the conversation and to probe E for elaboration of its meaning, whereupon in turn 04 E explains his meaning. A similar pattern develops in the subsequent turns, where R (in turn 05) once again focuses on E's introduction of a new idea. R says, "There was this suspicion?" which serves as a prompt for confirmation of the prior statement. Hence in this interchange we see R's manipulation of thematic formulations as a means for extending and directing the reporting activities of the respondent. Such topic management is common in elite oral history interviews, giving the oral historian an effective means for achieving coherence and elaboration of the subject matter under discussion.

A second topic management device—the cooperative recycle—is a means for the interviewer to restate the interviewee's prior talk. The restatement functions as a request for confirmation. In this way, the interviewer gives the interviewee an opportunity to affirm, deny, or represent the prior report. The following excerpt illustrates the cooperative recycle in use.

In this instance, the topic is a former congressman's decision to retire from politics.[24]

(01) R: Now on the **wings** of either political party there are those who would say that is the Establishment. Were you a part of the Establishment?

(02) E: I don't think there was any question that I was part of the Establishment, very decidedly. I am not sure what you mean by the wings!

(03) R: Well, the right wing of the Republican party, the left wing of the Democratic party.

(04) E: Oh, I don't consider myself the **right** wing of the Republican party!

(05) R: No, I mean most of the critics.

(06) E: [Oh.]

(07) R: Those are the people who would say this.

(08) E: Well, I think that there's no question that I was part of the Establishment. What I did find of particular interest was the way in which Democrats and Republicans could work together. It was my increasing **disillusionment** about this process that contributed to my decision to retire! Again I was not of an age where it was necessary for me to **retire**, but when we first went to Washington there was a feeling that cooperation was a good idea! I think the magic was that we had a Republican in the White House who could control some of the excesses that the Democrats in Congress might be ((uh)) trying to put across. If there were ideas that clashed too sharply with Eisenhower's feelings, nothing would be done. So there was a feeling that if you worked together you would get results. The whole business of what should be the responsibility of the Federal Government in the field of **education** was developed on that basis. There was an awareness that more needed to be done on the part of Republicans as well as Democrats. Obviously there were some Republicans you say the right wing that thought there was no business ((uh)) the Federal Government should not be getting in that business at all! but under the leadership of Democrats, somewhat reluctant leadership in the case of Graham Barden, on occasion, who was the chairman at the time, programs were developed which I think laid a foundation for a reasonable role for the Federal Government. I enjoyed very much in trying to get this movement, to give it some momentum. Graham Barden, I think, was a fascinating case study in himself because he was a conservative North Carolinian who had a good deal of charm and a good deal of force. And for years he was able to dominate the Democrats subordinate, junior, to him and there was a sort of informal working relationship with **Republicans** that allowed him to maintain control for as long as he did! And yet it at times got out of hand, and he would ((uh)) start a discussion of a Federal aid to education bill and then walk off the floor! because basically he was not enthusiastic about what was being advocated. Of course, **eventually** the Democrats on the committee realized that it was not necessary to subordinate themselves and kow tow to him and they in effect threw him over. It was a very interesting ((uh)) balance of power for a while and then a power struggle! It was really not until

Adam Clayton Powell became chairman that I got increasingly disillusioned with the **process**! because Adam Powell had a wonderful **opportunity** to build as an activist chairman and develop reasonable programs, and in **my** opinion, he was a poor chairman! Carall D. Kearns of Pennsylvania was the senior Republican at the time and I remember we used to stage some demonstrations outside of **Powell's door** because the Republicans were being totally **excluded** from Democrats' consideration about what should be done in committee. We thought that this was **wrong** and that we should be continuing to cooperate as we had in the past. It's not really **surprising** I don't suppose that the majority party runs the show but it became **painfully** obvious under Powell's leadership whereas before we had been given a more active role and a greater degree of responsibility. And so it was this feeling of frustration **with the process** and a failure to get along with Powell that led me to decide that my work on the Committee on Foreign Affairs was considerable and that I couldn't really devote enough time to it, and I **volunteered** to get off of Education and Labor.

(09) R: When you say, the increasing disillusionment with this process led you to retirement, ((uh)) do you mean ((uh)) disillusionment ((uh)) over the fact that the Democrats were beginning to exclude Republicans, would no longer work with them? Was that general throughout the Congress? [Cooperative Recycle/Request for Confirmation]

(10) E: I feel very strongly in the Foreign Affairs Committee that the Democrats **really** never gave the **time of day** to what might the committee usefully do at the next session. There was no question that we were out of that process. It was what **they wanted** and we had to jog along as best we could. And we had **serious** difficulty getting any kind of staff both on the Education and Labor Committee and then on the Foreign Affairs Committee? There was a feeling, in part, that the work of the committees was bipartisan and therefore you didn't need support which was quite obviously erroneous as far as **Education and Labor was concerned particularly**! If the staff was available for both, ((uh)) I feel that we should have been able to participate in what the staff should be doing. And so there was that feeling that you were, **at least I felt very strongly**, increasingly a fifth

wheel. There was less and less **a meaningful** contribution possible by the minority party.

Turn 08 displays the creative question-and-answer process of the oral interview method in that E answers an unasked question. This is accomplished by introducing his reason for deciding to retire within the topical context of bipartisian working relationships within Congress. In turn 09, R utilizes a cooperative recycle (also a request for confirmation) as a third-turn response to E. By so doing, R reformulates E's statement saying, "When you say, the increasing disillusionment with this process led you to retirement, ((uh)) do you mean . . . ?" R also directs E's next response with a follow-up question, "Was that general throughout the Congress?" By using the cooperative recycle coupled with a related follow-up question, R is able to confirm a particular interpretation as well as to direct the extension of the topic. Importantly, R does not assess or evaluate the answers supplied by E.

R is also able to maintain this neutrality to E and to the interview record by using an inferentially elaborative probe. This topic management device is a formulation that "commonly involves thematizing some presupposition of prior talk that the interviewer proposes is implied in that talk or its real world context."[25] The inferentially elaborative probe also functions as a request for confirmation.

In the following case, the topic is the 1964 Republican nominating convention for President of the United States.[26]

(01) R: Why did the New Jersey delegation split right down the line in the ((uh)) Goldwater and Scranton contest?

(02) E: Because there is that difference within the state I guess and especially among the delegates who get actually selected.

(03) R: [It wasn't a tactical move?]

(04) E: Oh, **no no**. It was just because we had this difference. We split right down the middle almost every time! I voted against Agnew at the '68 convention, which again was no foresight on my part, but it didn't seem to me that it was making any sense. I was not enormously enthusiastic about Nixon as a nominee and it did seem to me there

were better choices than Agnew who was an unknown figure, of course, I was appalled at Bill Miller being chosen. The process is a strange one. I was appalled really at Bob Dole being chosen because it didn't seem to me that it added any particular strength to the ticket.

(05) R: Those are the choices of the presidential nominee? [Inferentially Elaborative Probe/Request for Confirmation]

(06) E: Yes, presumably in every case it is! and I don't know whether Ford did his choosing because he wanted to placate but I don't think it placated anyone, and it certainly didn't add much variety or strength to the ticket.

This segment opens with a question about the New Jersey delegation's vote in the Goldwater and Scranton contest. E answers the question by explaining that state preferences and delegate preferences might represent two different perspectives. E expands the topic somewhat by expounding on his preferences in later conventions, particularly with regard to vice-presidential choices. He expresses his lack of regard for the choices historically made by the Republican presidential nominees. At this point in the interview, R utilizes an inferential elaborative probe (turn 05) to request confirmation of his conclusion, "Those are the choices of the presidential nominee?" E grants the request and confirms R's inference. Later on in the same interview, another inferentially elaborative probe is used by R.

This time the topic is the House of Representative's role in national foreign policy in light of the interviewee's visit to India and East Pakistan.[27]

(01) R: Did you circulate that report in the State Department? Did you have direct conversations with anyone in the State Department about the situation?

(02) E: I surely did. **I surely did!** I was terribly upset when I came back, and I must say, as an interesting sidelight on history because I don't think I've said it in news letters, I found the most responsive audience in the CIA because I came back, as I say, absolutely **appalled** at what I'd seen and anxious for someone to debrief me as they say. I did not find as much interest really in the State Department as I

had expected but I did find that the CIA were only too anxious to gather together and listen to me and ask questions. But, it was an enormously interesting experience and one that I think **we should be made to do**. We talk perhaps too much about Korea, but I went to Korea with ((uh)) (3.50) you know the Speaker who has now retired.

(03) R: The Speaker of the House? [Prompt Request for Confirmation]

(04) E: Yes.

(05) R: Albert? [Inferentially Elaborative Probe/Request for Confirmation]

(06) E: Albert, Carl Albert. Imagine not remembering his name, It's on the tip of my tongue. He'd never been out of the country before. And I think Rayburn took **pride** in the fact that he had never been out of the country. I **think** with our responsibilities we should be **made** to go out and I am sure it must have been a good thing for Albert to get out and see for himself what the Koreans are like, and to go up to the DMZ and ((uh)) sort of get some **feel** of the situation. It's the kind of thing that I think makes us keeps us provincial and we've got world responsibilities whether we like them or not. It's this kind of thing that got me **very restless** because as I say, I didn't feel that I was making any real contribution to the committee. ((uh)) They certainly were showing their ability to proliferate staff and to develop all sorts of interests, but it still didn't seem to me that we were developing any more impact on what was done, developing any more stature, any more respect as a committee than we'd had before, It always was somewhat lightweight, somewhat suspect, You automatically expect them to approve a foreign aid bill that everybody knows is too big, that sort of thing. Charlie Halleck was you know typical of the lack of respect that the committee got and he was not about to ((uh)) add people that he thought were going to change that situation.

(07) R: Well this would inevitably then prevent the House from playing a significant role in foreign policy? [Inferentially Elaborative Probe/Request for Confirmation]

(08) E: Well it can certainly cause **trouble**. It certainly can cause trouble.

Building upon the prior answer, R draws a conclusion on what he believes has been implied by E in turn 06. Turn 07 is used to formulate that conclusion and calls for affirmation or denial on the part of E, which is given in turn 08, "Well, it can certainly cause trouble." This sequence clearly demonstrates how inferentially elaborative probes, which serve simultaneously as requests for confirmation, can be used to move the topic beyond explicit answers to conclusions based on those answers. Even so, this topic management device allows R to remain neutral with regard to the interviewee and the record.

Whereas propositional coherence refers to the relatedness of utterance topics, pragmatic coherence refers to the relatedness of illocutionary acts and of their associated perlocutionary effects. In conversation, people have certain goals to achieve. Illocutionary acts—what is done in the act of saying—are the primary vehicles used to reach those goals. In addition, perlocutionary effects refer to the effects achieved by the speech actions. For example, in the context of a cocktail party, the hostess says to the sole remaining guest, "What time is it?" The guest responds "It is 1:30 and I must be leaving," and the guest departs. In this example, the speaker's question has the illocutionary force of suggesting that it is time to leave. By acknowledging the speech action and saying "It is time to leave," the hearer demonstrates "uptake" and indicates an understanding of the speaker's intention. The act of departing would be the perlocutionary effect. The overall scene illustrates that a politeness norm has been adhered to while achieving the goal of suggesting that the guest leave.[28] Such functional moves are common in discourse. The moves are necessary by virtue of metarules that sanction criteria such as politeness and relevance. Pragmatic coherence, then, refers to the local and global relatedness of illocutionary acts and to the relatedness of the associated perlocutionary acts.

Jacobs and Jackson maintain that cooperativity is a principle that conversationalists follow in order to achieve goals such as complimenting, cajoling, flattering, promising, and requesting.[29] Even an argument, Jacobs and Jackson say, is accomplished within this framework. The interlocutors must agree to disagree and must show one another that they are adhering to the accepted rules for managing arguments. From this viewpoint, then, the coherence of illocutionary acts and their associated perlocutionary effects is judged on the ability to achieve cooperativity as well as any other relevant subgoals achieved through substantive moves and management moves.

Discourse analysts are concerned with both direct and indirect substantive illocutionary acts. "Substantive moves make up . . . the subject matter of conversation, or the pragmatic topics that will be recalled subsequent to disengaging, such as that requests were made and granted, that compliments were given and accepted, and so forth."[30]

Direct substantive speech acts are those in which the literal interpretation is the intended interpretation. For example, the expression "I promise to be there at noon" accomplishes the performance of a promise in the act of saying the words. In conversation, therefore, the goal of displaying coherence and its overriding principle of cooperativity can be accomplished through the use of direct substantive speech acts.[31] The interpretive and performative rules that govern these speech acts are the subjects of myriad research projects.[32] The point here, however, is that an explanation of conversational coherence at the functional level involves direct substantive speech acts.

Similarly, an explanation of pragmatic coherence involves indirect substantive speech acts. These are illocutionary acts in which there is more to their substance than the literal interpretation. Here the notion of cooperativity with the related notion of saving face (i.e., being polite, being tactful) comes into play.[33] Indirect speech acts appear to be utilized when the speaker believes that the performance of a direct act would jeopardize the appearance of cooperativity and politeness. In other words, indirect illocutionary acts are used whenever there is a risk involved in using a direct illocutionary act. For example, the utterance "Don't you think it is time to leave?" is an indirect way of securing uptake as opposed to the utterance "Get your coat. We're leaving."

I believe that a norm of politeness or saving face or tact is central to elite oral history discourse. This is because elite respondents very often already have a public persona that they are interested in maintaining. In North American culture, being tactful is an important factor of image maintenance. Second, the fact that oral history interviews are conducted for an imagined audience makes the politeness expectation a public concern. In other words, the choices that might be made in private conversation are less constrained than the choices made for talk that is or could be public.

Management moves in conversation are considered essential to the accomplishment of pragmatic coherence. "Management moves . . . do not contribute new elements either to the pragmatic topic or to the incrementation of the propositional context set. Rather, they serve as a means by which parties provide one another with "benchmarks" so that they know where they have been, conversationally, and also where they are going."[34] Interlocutors must show that they are engaging in orderly behavior that adheres to the expectations of the social system. The talkers signal to one another where they have been and where they are going in the conversation. These signals facilitate interpretation and comprehension, particularly in lengthy or complex dialogues. Discourse analysts identify management devices and their usage rules in order to understand language in use. For example, "formulations" are devices used to place sequences of talk or episodes into a larger organizational framework. A formulation, then, may be a summary of what was just said by one's partner. "Gist" and "upshot" are formulations that render interpretations of preceding talk. Additionally, formulations may serve to terminate an episode of talk.

"Bracketing" is another organizational device that serves to mark out units of discourse. "While the global function of a discourse bracket is to organize talk into manageable chunks, the brackets may be observed to fulfill such specific subfunctions as *labeling* a section of talk (as a funny story, reason, or example) . . . *separating* one discourse unit from another . . . or *instructing* the hearer as to the illocutionary point of a forthcoming act."[35] In addition, even larger units of discourse are analyzed in terms of organizational management. Stories and arguments, for example, receive attention in terms of opening and closing devices, insertion sequences, and the like.

Clearly, the research foci in discourse analysis are too numerous to mention here, and excellent overviews of research can be found elsewhere.[36] The importance of investigating conversational coherence for understanding language in use, however, is relevant. My contention, of course, is that discourse performed in the hermeneutical situation of the oral history interview is rational action, and as rational action it should be examined using principles that are designed for application to purposive behavior. Discourse analysis provides just such a framework. The framework enables one to focus on language in use or language as action. Furthermore, the ways in which interlocutors display appreciation for and adherence to the need for conversational coherence can provide information about how meaning is constructed and negotiated during the course of interaction. These are the kinds of insights that can contribute to an understanding of the relationship between the process and the product of elite oral history. By focusing on the production and management of pragmatic coherence in the interview, one can begin to tap the meaning construction process that results in the oral text of oral history. This understanding, in turn, can serve as foundation for the development of criteria for evaluating the oral text as a source of historical evidence.

Requests

Intrinsic to the oral interview method is the class of illocutionary acts known as requests. This includes requests for action, information, clarification, confirmation, elaboration, etc. In the majority of interviews examined, requests comprise the bulk of illocutionary acts initiated by the interviewer. The speech action of making requests and the associated responses (grant/refuse) form the basis for the interview interaction. As indicated earlier, a central question is how interviewees simultaneously achieve their goals (e.g., the respondent may want to reveal as little as possible about a particular topic), deal with requests for information about the topic, and display cooperativity in the interaction.[37]

One of the most common types of requests is the request for information. In fact, the request for information governs the oral history interview process in that the purpose of the interrogation is to elicit information about the respondent's lived-through experience.[38] Interviewer utterances are interpreted within the framework "rule of request for information." A request for information is heard as valid by the interviewee if the interviewee believes: that the question is pertinent to the lived-through experience; that the interviewee has the ability and the obligation to provide the information; and that the interviewer has the right to ask for such information.[39] What actually happens, however, is that each question has the potential to be heard by the respondent as an indirect request for information.[40] This is because the contextual ground of the interview as an interrogation (a request for information) entails such a hearing. One result, for example, is that the interviewee extends the answer to include more themes or topics than those suggested by the question itself. Such interaction exemplifies how meanings and topics are negotiated through the question-answer complex and how the respondent plays a significant role in directing the flow of the talk. The following episode illustrates this process.

This excerpt is from an interview with a newspaper correspondent about the presidential campaign of John F. Kennedy.[41]

(01) R: ((uh)) Do you recall ((uh)) at what time or what period you began to consider Senator Kennedy worthy of wider coverage in terms of his ((uh uh)) goals in seeking the presidency? [Request for Information]

(02) E: ((uh)) Well, actually, I was willing to consider him seriously ((uh)) as a possibility at that first **luncheon**. The only reason for it is something that's very subjective. I think you'll probably find this true of most of us. I liked him, you know, kind of liked the cut of his jib. I didn't then think that a ((uh)) Catholic was going to be that it was going to be easy for a Catholic to run for the presidency, but I was hopeful that it might **happen** because, you know, I was hopeful that we'd get over that barrier in American political life. But, no, I can't say that I thought at the time that he was ((uh)) going to be a serious contender. But the evening of the **dinner** I spoke about, of the mixed American and foreign correspondents' group, ((uh)) I realized one thing then that he was a determined **young** man, and that he was going to make a run for the roses, as we say. ((uh)) It was going to take an awful lot to **deflect** him because he had given a **great deal** of thought to **every** aspect of his own position. The

Catholic aspect was foremost in his own account, or recital, of his shortcomings. But that doesn't really respond to your question. It's when I thought he was worthy of wider coverage! When he started going around the country as he did, meeting with governors and county courthouse politicians and so on, lining up delegates I don't remember at what point that was exactly in terms of a date or time but then it was clear he was worthy of wider coverage.

There was one brief moment in which he took me by surprise personally, and I think this may bear on your point a little bit. I went to either a press conference that he had or maybe it was the day he announced that he was a candidate I don't remember but as we were going out of the room I went over just to **reintroduce myself** because I didn't think you know, these fitful encounters we had that he would remember me. And he did. He called me by my first name, and he asked me, "How is **Sarge doing?**" "How is the Sargent doing" or "How is Sarge doing?" And I thought he was talking about some army sargeant [sic] that we may have known in common, and I was taken completely aback and I mumbled something like "Okay, I guess." Well, because I was a Chicago newspaperman, he thought I knew everything that **Sargent Shriver, his brother-in-law, was doing in Chicago!** . . . [Grant]

(03) R: ((uh)) During this time, were you ever approached by John Kennedy or his staff? about any articles you had written or were about to write? [Request for Information]

(04) E: No. Never. [Grant]

(05) R: Did he comment on any articles? [Request for Information]

(06) E: No. I never knew his staff, actually, during this period. I did know that there was a Ted Sorensen up there. I came to know that there was a Pierre Salinger there, but I think I sought him out rather than the other way around. My own more intimate relations and that's not a good word because I never really became an intimate, but my closer relationship didn't develop until after the campaigning got under way. [Grant]

In essence, both interviewer and interviewee are aware of the relationship between establishing validity of the interrogator's questions or requests for information and the expectation of an appropriate response by the interviewee. In fact, the respondent in turn 02 brackets and labels the prior response, saying, "But that doesn't really respond to your question." The informant then proceeds to attempt to provide a more direct response to the question. Later in that same turn, the respondent again brackets and instructs the interviewer on the illocutionary point of the forthcoming act, saying "and I think this may bear on your point a little bit." These statements are examples of the "management moves" that interlocutors utilize to signal, among other things, that they are being cooperative. Despite the fact that the expectation of being interrogated is intrinsic to the oral interview form, each participant interprets and performs the particular series of the utterances in relation to the rule of requests. The above episode, therefore, is an example of how what appears to be a direct request for information is interpreted and negotiated as an indirect request for information.

The following episode illustrates how a request for confirmation can be interpreted as an indirect request for information by the interviewer, with the interviewee hearing the request as valid and responding by granting the request. Note that the interpretation is grounded in the context of the interview itself, which thus far has centered on campaign experiences by the interviewee. Hence interpretation of speech acts and subsequent negotiation of meaning are related to the performance context itself.

(01) R: You traveled with Nixon as well during the '60 campaign. [Request for Confirmation/Indirect Request for Information]

(02) E: Yes, I traveled with Nixon. My basic travel with Nixon was on the train trip he took from Washington to, I think, Chicago or Detroit. I forget now. But through Ohio, mainly through Ohio where I think he campaigned very badly. I've often thought that those who accuse the press of being pro-Kennedy ((uh)) missed the point. We **really** showed a Nixon bias even though no one was particularly friendly to Nixon. The reason for the Nixon bias was simply that we didn't report how **badly** he campaigned. We were **afraid** to do this for fear that they'd say we were **biased** against him. So not reporting that, we showed **a bias** for him, really. I know

this is an unorthodox view, but I hold it, and I think I could make a small case for it anyhow. [Grant]

(03) R: Why did Nixon campaign badly? [Request for Elaboration]
(04) E: I don't know. . . . [Refuse]
(05) R: Did his antipathy to the press come across at that time? [Request for Confirmation]
(06) E: Well, yes, I think in small ways. . . . [Grant]
(07) R: Did this attitude reflect itself in his staff?[42]

In turn 01 of the episode, the interviewer utilizes the shared knowledge of the interlocutors of the rule of indirect request and the rule of request for confirmation to fish for information from the respondent. In this way, the interviewer avoids leading the respondent in any particular direction and provides the opportunity for the interviewee to interpret the content of the question in a broad manner. This episode is especially interesting because the flexible response in turn 02 becomes the basis of the subsequent question in turn 03, "Why did Nixon campaign badly?" and of a sequence of exchanges about the Nixon campaign style. Clearly, these exchanges represent how meaning is jointly constructed during the interaction. Furthermore, it appears that indirect requests for information are useful tools for facilitating a "flexible response," to use Thompson's term, on the part of the interviewee.

In the following excerpt, an associated interpretive rule comes into play. This is the rule of indirect request for permission to provide information.[43] This rule becomes operative whenever the respondent desires to include information into the interview record while acknowledging the interviewer's situational control over the line of questioning. Consider the following utterance (turn 01) as performing the illocutionary act of an indirect request.

(01) E: I'll **never forget** Dean Acheson's reaction to that! [Indirect Request to Provide Information]
(02) R: What was it? [Grant][44]

Note that in this instance, the interviewee would not have been free to include the information if the interviewer had not granted permission. So the statement in turn 01 is used as an indirect request to provide information that has not been solicited by the interviewer. By responding to the request with a related question, the interviewer grants the request, thereby turning control of the floor over to the interviewee. It appears that the rule of indirect request for permission to provide information functions prominently in the oral interview situation in which the interviewer, by role definition, has more control than does the interviewee. In other words, the interviewee has to rely on indirect means for inserting material into the record. The rule governing the procedure of the interview itself mitigates against free insertion of subjects by the respondent. Furthermore, the overriding goal of pragmatic coherence as well as the norms of politeness and relevancy inhibit direct assumption of control of the floor by the interviewee; that is, the interviewee is constrained by role and by the interview situation. Thus the interviewee is forced to negotiate control of the floor by the use of an indirect request for permission to provide information. In this way, the goals and subgoals of both parties are satisfied along with satisfying the overriding goal of pragmatic coherence—cooperativity.

Another type of request prevalent in the oral history interview is the request for confirmation.[45] This request for confirmation usually occurs in the form of a statement about a feature of the topic. The statement is heard, however, as a request for confirmation of the statement. That such illocutionary acts achieve the perlocutionary effect of confirming the statement is evidenced in the following exchange.

(01) R: Between 1948 and 1952, it seems that the party was built up to the position where it was strong enough to withstand the Eisenhower tide of '52, at least on the local offices. [Request for Confirmation]
(02) E: Yes. [Grant][46]

In fact, the reponse very often is in the form of yes or no, thereby indicating that the informant hears the statement as a yes-no question. Consider the following exchange from the same interview:

(01) R: Those years were years of intensive battles within the labor movement over the issue of Communism and anti-Communism. [Request for Confirmation]

(02) E: Yes. [Grant]

(03) R: Did that have any effect within the district? [Request for Clarification]

(04) E: I was not able to perceive that it had any really appreciable effect in that respect. There was, of course, the battle within the electrical worker's union at that time but it seems to me that perhaps both factions then supported the party. [Grant]

(05) R: You were active in the formation of the ADA. [Request for Confirmation]

(06) E: Yes. [Grant]

In this example, note that the two statements (turns 01 and 05) are heard as requests for confirmation whereas the question in turn 03 is heard as a request for clarification. That interlocutors are able to produce and interpret such different speech actions and that they are able to coordinate such production and interpretation indicate their depth of shared knowledge about the relationship between paralanguage and pragmatic coherence in conversation. In fact, there is no hesitation, no pause to consider the illocutionary and perlocutionary intent of the statements and the question. Rather, the interaction flows naturally as if all of this illocutionary work is being accomplished in a straightforward manner. As will be shown later, the rule of request for confirmation plays a significant role in other structural variations of elite oral history discourse, especially in hermeneutical conversation.

A final type of request found in elite oral history interviews is the embedded request.[47] An embedded request occurs whenever the interviewee responds to a request for information with a request. The request by the interviewee is heard as stating that more information is needed from the interviewer in order to respond. This rule is illustrated in the following sample.

(01) R: Back in those years when you were in the State Department, did you have much contact with Secretary [Dean] Rusk? [Request for Information]

(02) E: You mean when he was Assistant Secretary for Far Eastern Affairs? [Embedded Request]
(03) R: Right. [Grant]
(04) E: Not too much at that time. [Grant][48]

Here turn 02 serves as the embedded request for confirmation of the utterance in 01. Confirmation is provided in turn 03. Having obtained the information requested, the informant continues by answering the original request for information displayed in turn 01. Exchanges such as this are quite common in the interchange between interviewer and interviewee. In addition, it seems that the embedded request is compelling in its ability to secure uptake on the part of the interviewer. Moreover, an appropriate response by the interviewer is an essential ingredient of a successful interchange. The interaction could become nonsensical if the interviewer did not conform to the rule of embedded request.

Putting Off Requests

Unlike casual conversation where rights to ask questions and obligations to answer the questions are negotiated in terms of interactant relationships, the situation, the subject of conversation, and the like, the interview situation is interesting because of the presumption about interrogatories that are associated with the interviewer. By definition, the interview is an interrogation. Questions from the interviewer are expected and necessary to fulfill the goal of the interaction. Answers, of course, are expected from the respondent. In most cases, the presumption about validity of questions is very broad: as the person with most control of the floor, R is assumed to have the right to ask whatever is deemed necessary for the purpose of successfully completing the interview. This is done, of course, within the general framework of the cooperativity principle and its corollary maxims. At the same time, however, the interviewee must be able to, and frequently does, assert the prerogative for judging the appropriateness of a question. In other words, the interviewee may refuse to answer. The refusal, of course, must be accomplished within the general expectation of cooperation. The respondent must avoid being construed as recalcitrant, uncooperative, or hostile, especially because the interview is for the record. The respondent, therefore, must accomplish the joint goals of refusing and cooperating. Although these goals appear on the surface to be contradictory, closer examination reveals that illocutionary acts allow such goals to be integrated smoothly into the interaction. The question becomes one of determining how such a complex activity is accomplished. Here the rule of putting off requests[49] suggests that the interviewee can delay responding to a request for information by addressing the request itself in terms of timing and propriety. The interviewee also can question his or her ability and obligation to respond to the request.

Given the situational constraints on the interviewee in terms of obligation to respond, one would expect the rule of putting off requests to underlie a large portion of interview talk. In fact, this is the case. In the cases studied, the respondents are quite adept at refusing to answer while appearing to be cooperative. The following episode illustrates one variation of talk that invokes the rule of putting off requests. Here, the interviewee puts off the request until later, a form of indirect refusal.

(01) E: Newspapers in reporting this said that our word was they were going to kidnap Leibowitz and Brodsky and while we were concerned with them that they would mob lynch the blacks, Crowe told me there was never a word mentioned about the blacks. Didn't consider them. Well, I left a sergeant in charge.

(02) R: Did you talk to reporters about this incident? [Request for Information]

(03) E: I'll tell you **about that** as I come to it. I'd left one of my best sergeants at the jail in charge. [Refuse][50]

Of course, direct refusals also occur. In those instances, the respondent is obligated to provide some account for the refusal to answer. One reason for refusing to answer is lack of recall. Another reason for refusing the request for information is inability to answer; for example, "I don't know."

In the following example, the interviewer initially refuses

the refusal (turn 04), perhaps because the interviewee has indirectly introduced the topic in turn 01. So it is obvious that the informant remembers. Nevertheless, the respondent does not acquiesce (turn 05), and the interviewer ultimately drops the subject (turn 06).

(01) E: ... Maybe they went downhill a little bit because they didn't feel they had to necessarily have top rate candidates, and that they could elect damn near anyone they put up for it. In some instances I think some people who were put up were unfortunate.
(02) R: Anyone in particular? [Request for Information]
(03) E: Oh, I don't like to talk about it. [Refuse]
(04) R: Well, if there's any part of this that you don't want printed we'll just delete it. [Request for Information]
(05) E: I'd rather talk about that when the machine's off. [Refuse]
(06) R: Do you recall any issues that you as a congressman were particularly burned on?[51]

Summary

Interviews where the oral historian plays the role of information elicitor are common in oral history records. This chapter presents a description of the interpretive and performative strategies utilized by interviewers and interviewees to achieve cooperation and coherence in those single role situations. Maintenance of the role of information elicitor depends upon the interviewer's ability to move topic talk forward in a cooperative and coherent fashion while remaining neutral with respect to the informant's answers. Topic management devices such as the prompt predominate in such interview discourse. Requests are the predominant class of illocutionary acts used in such situations. The interpretive and performative rules for requesting information and for responding to a request have been discussed in terms of propositional and pragmatic (functional) coherence. The interviews examined involve oral historians and respondents who are competent managers of discourse in this type of interview situation. Their competence appears to depend upon the ability to achieve cooperation and coherence in an interrogatory situation.

3

Achieving Cooperation and Coherence in the Dual Roles of Information Elicitor and Assessor

(01) R: Okay. Let me move on now to the Buddhist crisis in the summer of 1963. This broke, I think, about May '63. You had the first business with the Buddhist flags being flown in a parade. What sort of impact did this have initially on Washington, before the self-immolations? [Request for Information]

(02) E: I think we recognized that there was a crisis coming up within the government which certainly could alienate popular support of the government. This we didn't like; we were trying to increase popular support. This was one of State's main endeavors, to increase popular support of the government. In the Buddhist crisis, we had a group of religious leaders who were trying to tear down that support. So we recognized it as a very serious situation almost from the beginning and tried to steer it so that the Vietnamese could calm it down. Again, I think in this particular crisis, there was a major difference of viewpoint between the Vietnamese and the Americans, of the understanding of how the other thought. Always, I would say, there was the interface between our democratic heritage and their rather autocratic heritage and way of life over the centuries. This is an important thing to understand, because they don't do things our way. They've never done them the way we do them. They have a much harsher outlook on life because

that has been their way of life. They don't have the independent way of looking at problems that we do. You have to take this into consideration. This goes back to a question you asked me before about a democratic form of government. A good democracy needs to have participation by all the people—active participation, that is. And this is sometimes difficult to get. [Grant/Assertion]

(03) R: All right. It's been said in defense of Diem, for instance, that here he was, a mandarin, in effect, and that to insist on his having popular support was somehow to make him lose this quality of leadership that was traditional in that area. [Request for Confirmation/Disputable Assertion]

(04) E: I don't agree with that. [Refuse/Deny]

(05) R: You don't? [Mitigated Challenge/Prompt]

(06) E: No. [Defend]

(07) R: Why not? [Mitigated Challenge/Prompt]

(08) E: Because we certainly tried to, . . . well, we felt that if we could increase popular support of the government, certainly the government could then take more effective measures in its own defense. This was not something that you could attain by direct military force. It had to be fought on the ground of having the people solidly behind you, of having the people work for the government, believe in and have confidence in the government, have the government provide security and have the people, again, participate in that effort. [Defend/Assertion]

(09) R: Yes. . . . [Accept][1]

In contrast with the previous chapter dealing with interviews where the interviewer maintained the role of information elicitor, this chapter focuses on interviews in which the interviewer enacts dual roles: information elicitor and assessor. One difference in the two interview situations is that the respondent and the record remain unchallenged in the former, whereas the record and the respondent are openly challenged in the latter. The interviewer not only evaluates the interviewee's answers but also introduces alternative interpretations for the interviewee's commentary. By so doing, the interviewer implicitly challenges the interviewee. The excerpt above illustrates these dual roles. In turn 03, the interviewer formulates a request for confirmation of an alternative interpretation of the subject, that is, a disputable assertion.

The respondent replies (turn 04) by refusing to confirm that interpretation. The interviewer subsequently prompts the respondent for clarification of his position, and the respondent complies with the request.

A second difference between these interview situations is seen in the interviewer's relationship to the imagined audience. In one, the oral historian remains neutral with respect to the imagined audience, allowing the audience to judge the emerging record. In the other, the oral historian who enacts dual roles evaluates the record for the imagined audience. Such assessment does not preclude further evaluation by the imagined audience. Such assessment, however, potentially influences the direction of subsequent evaluations, and it expands the topical domain open to evaluation. Differences in tone and style of the two interview situations are due to the fact that the interviewer and the respondent utilize additional discourse management devices during the course of the interchange. In particular, the interviewer's use of the third-turn response plays an important function in the enactment of the dual interviewer roles.

I have argued so far in this book that transformations of oral history conversation depend upon how the conversation is managed at the propositional and functional levels by both parties. In situations in which the interviewer enacts the dual roles of information elicitor and assessor, there are two possible outcomes. One is contradiction wherein "each interactant affirms her or his own perception of the historical event which, in turn, results in disagreement." Contradiction "represents the reification of the articulated conflict of perspectives, including those instances when one party acquiesces to, but does not accept, an account by the other party."[2]

The other possible outcome is contrariety, the actualization of the dialectical potential of the interchange. "Contrariety occurs when both interviewer and interviewee maintain their separate understandings, interpretations, and meanings of any feature of the event while acknowledging the potential validity of the other's perception."[3] In this section, the achievement of cooperation and coherence will be considered in terms of both outcomes of the articulated conflict: contradiction and contrariety.

Theoretically, articulated conflict is the prerequisite for transforming routine interview conversation into a conversation that is potentially dialectical. At the propositional level of discourse, articulated conflict is operationally defined as the display of differing points of view in the adjacency pair structure of conversational turns. In the former example, articulated conflict at the propositional level emerges in turns 03, 04, and 05, as the interviewee says, "I don't agree with that," and the interviewer responds, "You don't?"

At the functional level of discourse, articulated conflict is operationalized as the "withholding . . . of a preferred second pair-part and the failure to withdraw or suppress the disagreeable first pair-part" in the adjacency pair structure of conversational turns.[4] The same interview episode displays the emergence of functional conflict. Here, R (in turn 05) uses a mitigated challenge to call on E to admit or to defend the challenge. E (in turn 06) defends against the challenge. Because the preferred adjacency pair structure of a challenge is to admit rather than to defend the challenge, E's response displays conflict. Subsequent turns reinforce the conflict as R challenges the denial, saying "Why not?" E defends his position.

The question posed here is, how do interviewers and interviewees display cooperation while generating articulated conflict and transforming that conflict into either contradiction or contrariety? I argue that the disputable assertion is the primary propositional vehicle used by interviewers to elicit and assess the interview record. Likewise, I argue that the class of illocutionary acts known as challenges serves as the pragmatic vehicle in the emergence of assessed interview records. Prior to such consideration, however, selected substantive claims about the structure of conversational argument must be addressed. The purpose is to provide the background for showing that contradiction and contrariety (hermeneutical conversation) are special instances of conversational argument.

My position is that "the structure of conversational argument results from the occurrence of disagreement in a rule system built to prefer agreement."[5] Here the disagreement pertains to the incongruence of adjacent speech actions rather than to the substance of the propositions. Moreover, the adjacency pair—the fundamental organizational unit of conversation—is the key to that disagreement. Most adjacency pairs (e.g., question-answer, request-grant/refusal, challenge-admit/defend) display a "structural preference for agreement,"[6] wherein the first pair part (FPP) establishes a "next turn position which is expected to be filled by an appropriate second pair part (SPP)."[7] This means that the SPP is constrained by the FPP in that a certain SPP will be expected to occur. For example, because the preferred SPP of a request (FPP) is a grant, not a refusal, a request to be told the time (i.e., "Do you have the time?") is expected to be granted (i.e., "It is two o'clock."). Likewise, the preferred SPP of a challenge is to admit, not to defend. In fact, the normative preference for structural agreement in conversation is so strong that noncompliance must be accompanied by a plausible reason, such as inability to perform the preferred SPP. In the above example, therefore, to refuse the request to be told the time would require a plausible reason for refusing the request (e.g., "I don't have a watch.").

Arguments are disagreement relevant speech events; they are characterized by the projection, avoidance, production, or resolution of disagreement. Argument attends to the withholding, or potential withholding, of a preferred SPP and the failure to withdraw or suppress the disagreeable FPP. . . . Second, arguments appear as a variety of structural expansions of adjacency pairs. They may involve turn expansions or sequence expansions focusing on either pair part, but they occur within the interpretive frame provided by a dominant adjacency pair.[8]

From a pragmatic (functional) viewpoint, therefore, arguments pertain to turns in which there is disagreement, or incongruence, over the speech actions. The disagreement focuses on the appropriateness of the speech acts within adjacency pairs according to the governing rule system. Of course, from a propositional viewpoint, arguments can also be about what is said. Within this complex communicative situation, cooperation must be achieved. The following section, therefore, addresses the interpretive rules, the propositional devices, and the speech actions used for achieving cooperation and coherence in the hermeneutical situation of oral history when the interviewer enacts dual roles of elicitor and assessor. Special attention is given to two forms of discourse found in elite oral history: contradiction and contrariety (hermeneutical conversation).

As indicated earlier, articulated conflict is the precondition for the emergence of contradiction or contrariety. Articulated conflict occurs whenever one party withholds a preferred SPP and the other party fails to withdraw or suppress the disagreeable FPP. Examination of the interview data reveals that the request for confirmation is one type of speech act utilized by interviewers that creates the potential for articulated conflict to occur. For example, whenever a request for confirmation is granted, there is no conflict; whenever the request is denied—that is, disconfirmed—there is articulated conflict (the preferred structure of a request is a grant, not a refusal). Consider, for example, turns 11, 12, and 13 from an interview with a high-ranking military official in the Pentagon in 1970.[9]

(01) R: All right. What did you see in the way of a changeover in the way the new administration was coming in, ((uh)) from the top on down, from President Kennedy through Secretary McNamara and ((uh)) Paul Nitze and Bill Bundy? How were these people taking hold, what briefings were they given by the outgoing people, and this sort of thing, that you know of? [Request for Information]

(02) E: To my **knowledge**, each one coming in, each man in a political appointment, (3.29) went around to the various offices with which he was to be connected, the people that he had to work with, and was given a briefing by them ((uh)) he had a time to take over in his new job, although generally not for very long. In some cases there was a time for the appointee to ((uh)) work into his job while he was waiting for his **security** clearance. In general, however, I think the turnover was quite rapid and, as I recall, nearly all the political appointees were changed. [Grant]

(03) R: Now, how were these men taking hold of their jobs? What things were they beginning to do in the way of giving you and others on the staff ((uh)) ideas of how they wanted the operation in ISA to be run? Were there new things happening or was it the same thing over again? [Request for Information]

(04) E: To my recollection, there wasn't much of a change in our methods of operation. There were a few extra jobs created,

with only a small change in the organization within ISA. By and large, they had to grasp hold of the ongoing problems, work with them, and wrestle with them as did we. The military ((uh)) people in the Pentagon did not change at that time other than by the routine process, so that I didn't find any **great change** within ISA other than the new personal relationships that grew up with different people! For example, I got to know Paul Nitze. I hadn't known his predecessor too well since I hadn't been there very long. I got to know **Bill Bundy** who was quite a different man than Frank Sloan,

R: [uh huh]=

E: who as I recall held the job before him. They had different backgrounds, different personalities, but in general, they worked in much the same way.=

R: [uh huh]

E: =There was, I think, a tendency to take a firmer grasp of the problems by the White House. [Grant/Assertion]

(05) R: In what way? [Request for Clarification/Prompt]

(06) E: This is a feeling I have, and I'm basing this only on, say, two months ((uh)) of the outgoing administration, so you could expect them to have a type of ((uh)) holding position and not to commit the new administration.=

R: [uh huh]

E: =I would ascribe it more to this than anything else, other than the character of the president, of course.=

R: [uh huh]

E: =I think he did set up a stronger White House staff as such. I don't know too much about how the inner workings of government were under the prior administration. There was a change. I think the ((uh)) National Security Council type of paper tended to be downgraded, and it went to a more personal working relationship of the president and his senior advisers. [Grant/Assertion]

(07) R: uh huh, uh huh, Yes, I've heard this from other sources as well. [Accept/Confirmation]

(08) E: There used to be a set of regular National Security Council actions or memoranda which were the basis of actions within the government ((uh)) and a formal organization had been set up. This hadn't been working too well as I understand it and by and large this formal process tended to be degraded=

R: [uh huh]

E: = I would say it wasn't really resurrected until just recently in the last couple of years. [Continuation of Grant/Assertion]

(09) R: = There was no resurrection of it after? [Mitigated Challenge/Disputable Assertion]

(10) E: I think [Lyndon B.] Johnson tended to work more in this formal process. [Preemptive Defense/Assertion]

(11) R: I was thinking about the post Bay of Pigs because everybody sort of got caught off base after dismantling everything on that one. [Request for Confirmation/Disputable Assertion]

(12) E: **No, I don't have a feeling that they changed because of the Bay of Pigs.** =

R: [uh huh]

E: = **This was something that had been done. I wasn't in on the planning of that at all, but I got in when the action started just as a spectator.** [Refuse/Deny]

(13) R: Yes, how did you view it as a spectator? What recollections do you have of that? [Request for Information]

Turns 11 and 12 in this episode represent the production of articulated conflict. Turn 11 functions as a request for confirmation and a disputable assertion; turn 12 is the refusal—the disconfirming response. The result is articulated conflict. It is at this juncture in the dialogue that the conversation either becomes contradiction or has the potential to transform into contrariety. What emerges is dependent upon the interviewer's third-turn receipt. In this episode, contradiction is the emergent form as illustrated by turn 13 in which the interviewer uses the third-turn receipt to probe for information about a related topic rather than pursuing the disagreement-relevant speech act—the disconfirmation. Thus the record shows a state of contradiction between the interlocutors. As discussed earlier, however, it is possible that the interviewer's nonverbal cues signify agreement with the other's position. In other words, R continually expresses "uh huh" as E defends his position. The placement of these vocalic cues, as well as R's "Yes" at the beginning of turn 13, suggests that R understands (perhaps accepts) E's defense. Interchanges such as this should be examined carefully by users of oral history data because such scrutiny provides clues to the meanings constructed by the interlocutors. Clearly, the contextual grounding of the verbal and nonverbal cues plays significant roles in understanding the dialogue.

Contradiction and contrariety are also the possible outcomes of a class of speech acts known as challenges. In the oral history interview, the mitigated challenge is the speech act that has the illocutionary force to make problematic an utterance by E. "Mitigated challenges are utterances such as questions and assertions and the like which call into question E's interpretations of Z without questioning E's competence as an informed reporter of her or his lived-through experience."[10] Hence mitigated challenges implicitly affirm one of the preconditions for responding to a challenge to one's viewpoint—ability to respond. The mitigated challenge acknowledges the respondent's ability. Furthermore, mitigated challenges perform a preemptive function relative to the establishment of articulated conflict. The mitigated challenge preempts the need to articulate conflict in preceding turns because the challenge presupposes such conflicting perspectives. Articulated conflict is implicit within the turn.[11] Mitigated challenges, therefore, can serve dual illocutionary goals in the interview situation: to establish the conflicting perspectives and to make problematic a given interpretation.

In the following example (which was also presented at the beginning of this chapter), turns 03–09 display the emergence of contradiction via two mitigated challenges from the interviewer (turns 05 and 07). This sequence of speech actions can be depicted as request-refuse (turns 03–04), challenge-defend (turns 05–06), challenge-defend (turns 07–08). At the same time, turn 03 functions simultaneously as a disputable assertion and as a request for confirmation, meaning that the interviewer is inserting an alternative interpretation into the record for consideration by the respondent and the imagined audience. In this instance, the respondent rejects the alternative explanation while refusing the request for confirmation. The interviewer, however, does not follow up on this line of questioning. The result is contradiction and this time there are no supportive vocalic cues from R.

(03) R: All right. It's been said in defense of Diem, for instance, that here he was, a mandarin, in effect, and that to insist on his having popular support was somehow to make him lose this quality of leadership that was traditional in that area. [Request for Confirmation/Disputable Assertion]

(04) E: I don't agree with that. [Refuse/Deny]

(05) R: You don't? [Mitigated Challenge/Prompt]

(06) E: No. [Defend/Deny]

(07) R: Why not? [Mitigated Challenge/Prompt]

(08) E: Because we certainly tried to, well, we felt that if we could increase popular support of the government, certainly the government could then take more effective measures in its own defense. This was not something that you could attain by direct military force. It had to be fought on the ground of having the people solidly behind you, of having the people work for the government, believe in and have confidence in the government, have the government provide security and have the people, again, participate in that effort. [Defend/Assertion]

(09) R: Yes. . . . [Accept][12]

The next example also illustrates the emergence of contradiction after E initially refuses the request for confirmation (turn 02). R then utilizes a disputable assertion (turn 03) to probe for confirmation, E denies the assertion (turn 04), and R acquiesces (turn 05). In this episode, the timing of E's responses is noteworthy; that is, E's answer in turn 02 contains lengthy pauses. In North American English-speaking cultures, such lengthy pauses could mean that E is being careful, being deliberate, or being deceptive. Junctures like this remain puzzling for subsequent data users. One solution would be for the interviewer to insert comments about the interpretations of pauses at the time of interview. These comments could appear as marginalia in the final transcript. Of course, the audiotapes also provide clues to interpretation for all listeners.

(01) R: Okay, one or two more questions on Brazil. One is on the AID operation in support of training the police and so on. ((uh)) There's been some evidence that **since that** time that the CIA was heavily involved in this end of things. Were

they so in **Brazil**? operating under an AID cover? [Request for Confirmation/Disputable Assertion]

(02) E: (10.52) I couldn't say. There were some of them there, (2.56) but (4.32) they have a different mission, of course, and while CIA people sometimes work under cover with these various outfits, with AID and so on, they're doing their own job. They only do enough of the other stuff such as using the offices and so on. [Refuse/Hedged Denial]

(03) R: Well, **what I'm looking for, I think**, is that somebody somewhere along the line in doing research in the Kennedy library or doing research elsewhere is going to hit upon the idea that the CIA engineered the coup that came later! and one of the ways they did it was operating under an AID cover training the police and this kind of thing. To your knowledge, was any of this going on? [Request for Confirmation/Disputable Assertion]

(04) E: No. [Refuse/Deny]

(05) R: Okay. [Accept]

(06) E: I think that's ridiculous. [Continuation of Denial/Assertion]

(07) R: Okay, fine. Well, this is the kind of thing that is very **prevalent** nowadays I know and somebody is going to grab hold of it and try to make a case for it. And I'd like to have some evidence somewhere **one way or the other**, you know. [Request for Confirmation of Prior Disputable Assertion]

(08) E: Even the **Arabs** are charging the **CIA** with most of this stuff in Israel! I suppose they're in a difficult position because they would have to **deny it anyway**, but I'm quite sure that CIA and no other American for that matter had anything to do with Castelo Brance taking the leadership of that drive, you might call it a general's movement, to oust Goulart. [Continuation of Denial/Refuse][13]

In oral history interviews, conversational structures that are dominated by disputable assertions and mitigated challenges usually result from initiatives by the interviewer. This is because the role expectations associated with an oral interview commonly provide more opportunity for the questioner to be the challenger. (Indeed, some oral historians such as Grele argue that the pragmatic or functional goal of the oral historian is to challenge or to make problematic the individual story or narrative in order to transform the single experience into a cultural narrative.) In the interviews examined, contradiction emerges much more frequently than contrariety. In fact, the emergence of contrariety is rare relative to the quantity of interview dialogue examined. An interesting question, therefore, is why contrariety appears to be so elusive as an interview form? A related question is how do interviewers and interviewees display cooperation while engaging in dialogue that transforms into contrariety? In the next section, attention will be given to the accomplishment of cooperation and coherence within contrariety or hermeneutical conversation.

Hermeneutical Conversation

Hermenutical conversation as the art of engaging in a conversation is "also the art of seeing things in the unity of an aspect (*sunoran eis hen eidos*) i.e., it is the art of the formation of concepts as the working out of the common meaning."[14] "Precisely this," Gadamer observes, "is what characterizes a dialogue, in contrast with the rigid form of the statement that demands to be set down in writing: that here language, in the process of question and answer, giving and taking, talking at cross purposes and seeing each other's point, performs that communication of meaning which, with respect to the written tradition, is the task of hermeneutics."[15]

Turning, then, to my earlier question: Why is hermeneutical conversation so elusive as a conversational form in oral history interviews? I believe it is because there are socially unacceptable consequences, particularly for the public record, of admissions to challenges. The problem is that whenever conflict occurs there is an assumption that either R or E is wrong. Hence there is an inclination to save face by defending one's original position or answer.[16] The task here is to reveal the communication strategies used by interviewers and interviewees to transcend the social norms that constrain elite oral history interviews. Toward that end, episodes of hermeneutical conversation are examined. Here, special attention is given to the third-turn responses manifested as disputable assertions and mitigated challenges. Before proceeding, however, certain observations about disputability of events are significant for understanding the production of hermeneutical conversation in oral history interviews:

1. Making events disputable (i.e., both R and E acknowledge the potential disputability of their respective interpretations of the historical event) is a prerequisite for the emergence of contrariety transformed as corrected meaning or constructed meaning.
2. To make events disputable is to open up the potential for reinterpretation of the lived-through experience by one or both interactants.
3. Disputability of events is locally occasioned and retrospective in the conversational process.
4. Once interpretations of events have been classified as disputable, that state of disputability remains valid throughout the interview, that is, any subsequent interpretation can legitimately be disputed without having to engage in the discourse necessary for making events disputable.[17]

Two rules are sufficient for explaining how events are made disputable. The rule of admitting disputability of events[18] is central to the process of conversational management, enabling interactants to transform discourse from a state of conflict to a state of contrariety. The rule suggests that if an interviewer disputes an answer and if the interviewee responds to the challenge without taking exception to the interviewer's underlying assumptions, then the interviewee admits that the original answer is disputable. Whenever interpretations of events acquire this status of being disputable, then the rule of disputable assertions[19] becomes applicable. This means that any assertion about a disputable interpretation is heard as a request for the interviewee to give an evaluation of that assertion. These two rules can be seen operating in the following episode from an interview with a military official who served during the Kennedy administration.

In turn 07, for example, R makes a request for an evaluation of a disputable assertion about positions taken on the use of military assistance in foreign countries. In turn 08, after pausing 4.3 seconds, E admits the disputability of the assertion and proceeds to evaluate the assertion, thereby providing another viewpoint on the military intervention issue. Turn 09 is an inferentially elaborative probe in which R simultaneously requests confirmation of his inference: "Simply from the point of view of stability?" E uses turn 10 to affirm R's inference and to refute the earlier new left position on military assistance articulated in turn 07, saying "There was much more of this feeling than any idea of building up a military establishment because we thought they should have one, or that it's good to have one. I didn't find that at all." R uses turn 11 to present a related disputable assertion that Secretary McNamara meddled in State Department affairs. E affirms the assertion and provides the McNamara viewpoint on the issue (turn 12). These exchanges represent the negotiation of interpretations through the question and answer process. This episode also illustrates how disputable assertions can be used as probing devices and how vocalic cues such as "uh huh" that signify support can be used to move the dialogue forward in the direction desired by the interviewer. For example, despite the verbal disagreement over interpretations of the historical event in question, the interactants signal their cooperation through vocalic cues (and probably through nonverbal cues such as head nods and smiles). This kind of "living speech," to use Gadamer's term, is what enables a state of contrariety to emerge and to be sustained. This contextual grounding of oral interviews must be considered when evaluating the data obtained through the oral interview method.

(01) R: Okay, let me ((uh)) ask you about the relationships with other agencies, then. To what extent were you directly or indirectly in support of the National Security Council? and ((uh)) I'm particularly interested in whether there was a special relationship there, of course, with Bill Bundy and Mac Bundy. [Request for Information]

(02) E: Well, of course, you couldn't avoid a **direct** relationship between Bill Bundy and Mac Bundy. [Grant]

(03) R: Right. [Affirm]

(04) E: But ((uh)) (4.66) I don't know that this really affected the way things were handled. We worked very closely with State and had representatives from State in the Pentagon for various meetings, although more often I was over in **State** = .

R: [uh huh]

E: = and in connection with these problems we got to know

the AID people as well as the State Department people **rather well** because we always worked closely together. The military assistance and the economic assistance. We tried to mesh them as closely as we could although the objectives sometimes differed, country by country. [Continuation of Grant/Assertion]

(05) R: In what way? [Request for Clarification]

(06) E: Well (4.60) I thought of that when I said it, Now I've got to come up with an example. (laugh, cough) (8.74) The objective we had for military assistance varied from country to country. =

R: [uh huh]

E: = In some cases I would say there was almost purely a political rationale behind our military assistance; in other cases we were more interested in getting a better military organization. In Korea, for example, we wanted to have a strong military organization. In Burma we knew this wasn't possible and there we had more of a political rationale. =

R: [uh huh]

E: = In Cambodia it was more of a political rationale. When we got to Vietnam here we had our military political rationale. So it **changed** from country to country. Economic assistance I think always was very clearly looking for **economic improvement** in the country and it was meshed, for example, in Korea. In Vietnam, we were ((uh)) both working to stave off the rising insurgency there. =

R: [uh huh]

E: = I think there the administration tried to mesh them very closely and carefully. There's one thing. In looking back on it. I came in at the time that military assistance was on the downgrade =

R: [uh huh]

E: = excepting for Vietnam. So we were always closing **down** the throttle =

R: [uh huh]

E: = rather than opening it up, except for Vietnam, Thailand, and Laos. [Grant/Assertion]

(07) R: This is looked at on a couple of different levels; one, in the sort of new left position in which they look on ((uh)) any merger of military and purely economic assistance as a kind of devious, insidious ((uh)) attempt for the military to intrude into something that's not their **business**. At an-

other level, you have the interdepartmental jealousies, State believing that it **really understands** the situation, and Defense, on the other hand, **really understands** the situation. How much of this comes through in your dealing with it from the ISA end? [Request for Evaluation/Disputable Assertion]

(08) E: (4.3) Well, I was **somewhat** in the middle, in that we always had the JCS looking at military assistance more or less from a military viewpoint, State looking at it from the political viewpoint, and AID wondering how it was going to affect **their program**. Of course, in a certain way we and AID were competing, because military and economic assistance were in the same bill! I think that the people handling it in ISA had a good understanding of what the objectives were in every country and didn't look at it as a ((uh)) buildup of military influence. I think we would have liked to have had more influence in some countries because this would have helped the country **politically**. [Grant/Assertion]

(09) R: uh huh, Simply from the point of view of stability? [Request for Confirmation/Inferentially Elaborative Probe]

(10) E: Of stability? Well, where we could influence the military people, I think, by and large, we always tried to influence them toward a closer relationship with **the U.S.** because this would help **our country** in international relationships. =

R: [uh huh]

E: = We wanted to have say Indonesia on our side, a country of a hundred million people. =

R: [uh huh]

E: = Our country was interested in stability and in preserving the freedom of Southeast Asia and since in many countries the military are so **influential**, we thought it was to our best **U.S. interest** to have a good **rapport** with them. There was much more of **this feeling** than any idea of building up a military establishment because we thought they should have one it's good to have one. =

R: [uh huh]

E: = I didn't find that at all. [Grant/Affirm]

(11) R: What about back on the Washington end? ISA sometimes has been called the little State department and the question of whether or ((uh)) not Secretary McNamara was taking too many initiatives in foreign affairs, and so on, away from

The Dual Roles of Information Elicitor and Assessor / 69

what was normally State Department prerogatives and this kind of thing? How do you view that? [Request for Evaluation/Disputable Assertion]

(12) E: I think there's no question but what that McNamara got into areas which previously had been purely State Department business. He **did have** an influence on it, but he took the position again this is as it developed in his tenure that he was running an organization which had a budget of seventy or sixty billion dollars, whatever the number was at that time, and three and a half million people and certainly he would use it to the best interests of the United States in **whatever way he could, as the President** wished. [Grant/Affirm]

(13) R: All right, now did this have any reaction from the **State Department side** that you know of? [Request for Information]

(14) E: No, **I don't think so** because we did work very closely together! They always knew what we were doing. (7.36) We did, I think, in ISA have an **influence** on foreign policy because we were working so closely with the State Department. [Grant/Assertion]

(15) R: uh huh Okay. Now what I'm, looking for and really fishing for is a kind of identification of position by DOD [Department of Defense] and another by State that might be **different**, in which you came to some difference of opinion. [Request for Information]

(16) E: Well, there **were many**! =
    R: [all right]
    E: = Sometimes they were small, and sometimes they're large. I remember one of the early **differences** of opinion, and this is perhaps a minor matter. We gave Laos, as I recall something like six or eight T6 aircraft. =
    R: [uh huh]
    E: = They were old trainers. =
    R: [right]
    E: = They can carry all of about two one-hundred pound bombs. We **wanted them to use bombs**. We thought that would be most effective in stopping the Pathet Lao and State said no They didn't want to **use bombs**! [Grant][20]

The rule of disputable assertions is also displayed in the following exchange with another high-ranking military official. In fact, R uses turn 05 to introduce a disputable assertion about the relationship between the "whiz kids" of the McNamara Defense Department and the military command. E confirms the interpretation in turn 06. Once again, R participates paralinguistically in the exchange, setting a tone, or ambience, that is cooperative. Certainly access to videotapes of such exchanges would reveal additional cooperative cues.

(01) R: Let me ask you how people in the military, particularly in DOD in your area **looked** on the arrival of a new Democratic president, particularly President Kennedy? How did you see this? [Request for Information]

(02) E: As a normal change of government. =

R: [uh huh]

E: = I think that we saw it only as we may have voted. =

R: [uh huh]

E: = And if you voted for the opponent, you think it's bad; if you voted for him, it's good. I would say there's no other reaction than that. [Grant/Assertion]

(03) R: Okay, fine. How about Secretary McNamara? This is a little different. It affects people in DOD a little more directly. [Request for Information]

(04) E: Well, I can remember everybody wondering what he had done before and remembering the so-called "whiz kids." The major (6.86) problem that developed there was his own policy planning staff, the so-called "whiz kids" that he brought in, that gradually got so much internal power. They developed into the Office of Systems Analysis, wherein they would make their own analyses, then assume that they had the right answers and defy anyone in the military to disprove them. [Grant/Assertion]

(05) R: Was this, in fact, the real problem with him coming in? Because I've heard it from **both sides** now, and the whiz kids' side, of course, is that well, the military just doesn't understand the way we talk! If they'd **only learn our language**, perhaps they could appreciate that we've got a slightly different point of view. If they'd only **understand** it, maybe we'd get along better! And the military, of course, saying the same thing, that the whiz kids don't understand the military point of view. Now **where** does this all meet? or is it always a standoff? How do you work together? [Request for Confirmation/Disputable Assertion]

(06) E: I believe it's probably a standoff. =

R: [uh huh]
E: = Certain of these people came in with different back-
     grounds and new ideas, but it seems to me they started off
     assuming they knew **a lot more than they really did** =
R: [uh huh]
E: = and would take positions which frequently we thought
     just didn't quite ring true! But it was awfully hard to con-
     vince them that we, too, had a viewpoint. [Grant/Confirm]
(07) R: All right, what did you do in order to convince them? What
         sort of things did you find were effective? [Accept/Request
         for Clarification]
(08) E: (8.9) I would say that you would get a better answer on
         this one from someone who was in the JCS, rather than
         me. It didn't impinge too much on me at that time. [Re-
         fuse][21]

The next excerpt is an excellent example of how hermeneutical conversation arises through R's use of a third-turn
response (turn 03). This is a disputable assertion about the command relationship between the Military Assistance Command
and the Commander-in-Chief of the Pacific Command. E's response in turn 04 admits the disputability of the assertion and
transcends his personal view, saying "If there were any difficulty I would say it transpired because with a senior commander on scene, related especially to one service, it made it
a little stickier to get my problems heard at the highest level!"
E goes on to clarify the command problem, and the answer
provides insight into the command relationship in question.

(01) R: All right. Now how did things change over the course of
         the time that you were there? What were some of the sig-
         nificant developments as you saw them? [Request for In-
         formation]
(02) E: Overall the most significant one, I suppose, was the in-
         crease in size of the U.S. contingent out there! Equally, the
         steadily increasing **interest** by the United States **govern-
         ment** in Vietnam, which of course was just a follow-on to
         the decisions that the President had made as the effort
         gained momentum. This is almost true from the very be-
         ginning although the momentum built up as time went
         on! As to the organization in **country**, the major signifi-
         cant one of course was the establishment of the Military

Assistance Command, MACV, in February of 1962.
... Although COMUSMACV was officially established in
February of '62, it seemed to me that no effect of MACV
was felt until the following year, actually I would say about
the latter part of 1962. . . . [Grant/Assertion]

(03) R: MACV's a sort of **curious breed of cat**, isn't it? You've got
a four-star rank running the show, and yet he's subordinate
to CINCPAC, and yet he **really has** his line going all the
way back to Washington! How difficult was this command
relationship? [Request for Confirmation/Disputable As-
sertion]

(04) E: It did not cause any difficulty as far as I was concerned. If
there were any difficulty I would say it transpired because
with a senior commander on scene, related especially to
one service, it made it a little stickier to get my problems
heard at the highest level! As to the idea that you bring
up, I think that in **my mind** it amounted to something like
this, CINCPAC was back in Honolulu. He had many other
responsibilities around the Pacific area, and so in essence
in my mind anyway it was something like **that part of the
CINCPAC** organization that was focusing entirely on Vietnam had moved out to Saigon, and that was sort of the
way I rationalized MACV. There's no **question** it was a
one-over-one **command** situation which always seems to
be a peculiarity. . . . [Grant/Affirm][22]

In the next episode corrected meaning first emerges in turns
4–11 as interviewer and interviewee continue to explore the
distinctions between the military concepts of flexible response and variable force. Corrected meaning emerges again
as R uses a cooperative recycle to request confirmation of his
interpretation (turn 19). E affirms that view (turn 20).

(01) R: Okay, let me ask you something else about the special
forces and that is that with Kennedy coming in, and with
Maxwell Taylor coming in . . . the whole idea of the special
forces underwent **something of a change** I **think**, developing the counterguerilla warfare, counter insurgency business as opposed to this **earlier** idea. I do recall seeing in
one place that President Kennedy couldn't understand
quite **why special forces should be in Germany**. Why

weren't they out in the jungles of Vietnam or New Guinea or whatnot? He seemed to think this was the appropriate place for them rather than in Germany. Do you recall the situation at that time? [Request for Information]

(02) E: Yes, of course. To give you an answer, maybe, to Mr. Kennedy's question. They were in Germany because they were not going **to retire** when the rest of the forces withdrew to the Rhine! They were going up in these areas to which they were assigned! But this counterguerilla thing became a popular thing all along and it leads to something. [Grant/Assertion]

Do you want to ask any more questions about that special forces before I go on? [Topical Management Move]

(03) R: No, this was my last question. [Topical Management Reply]

(04) E: . . . But Mr. McNamara's first move when he took over as Secretary of Defense was to call for some studies about **how much army was needed**! And ((uh)) so we made such a study and put it in there to him. . . . In the meantime, he'd gotten some others started and the administration, **perhaps with Max Taylor's spurring**! or at least his advice, got moving very quickly on **building up** the army. And it was fortunate that they did! This counterguerilla thing was a **development** of a scheme which I think Max originated to have forces that would allow the President to move where anything was required! from an MP to a nuclear weapon! so that in between there he had freedom to do something and countering guerillas was one of the **things** in there. If you remember Max made a much quoted statement to the effect that if a sniper got up in a church steeple we had to have some way to get him **out** other than destroying **the church, the bishop**, and **diocese**! So he was pushing this scheme of his! And I **forget what he called it**. He might have called it variable force or something like that! The reason I mention it to you is to make **very clear** the difference between what I will call variable force, though that was not his language, and the so called = [Continuation of Grant/Assertion]

(05) R: = Flexible response. [Request for Confirmation/Inferentially Elaborative Probe]

(06) E: Huh?

(07) R: Flexible response.

(08) E: It's not the same. That's the point I'm making. [Refuse/Deny]

(09) R: No. All right. Fine. [Accept]

(10) E: Yeah. It's two different things. [Disputable Assertion]

(11) R: Okay. [Accept]

(12) E: [Now, the difference has gotten lost. This business of the flexible response first appeared while I was in Sec. Def's office as a study from Rand Corporation. Rand Corporation was under contract to the Department of the Air Force to make studies, but their contract permitted them to **originate** some things now and then, and they **originated this one**! The object of the thing was to **avoid provoking the enemy**! into nuclear attack by keeping these wars on a small scale. You kick me in the shins, I'll kick you in the shins. You hit me in the nose, I'll hit you in the nose. Well, it was a manner of making war which no military type has ever **believed in**! We had always thought from Clausewitz on that the way to fight a war was to get in and win it, end it, not this **drawn out** thing. I saw the thing when it came into DOD, but it seemed so ridiculous to me I didn't say anything about it! let it go along. By that time Nitze was gone and Bundy was out of there, but McNaughton and some of those fellows in ISA, they **loved this thing**! And I **suppose** Mr. McNamara **loved** it although he never talked to me about it. But as you know, the **present war** has been conducted under that theory. [Disputable Assertion]

(13) R: How is this different from what you were talking about, the variable force thing? [Mitigated Challenge/Disputable Assertion]

(14) E: We were talking about developing a **capability** of meeting threats without having, **on our part**, **to use the nuclear weapon**! And every military man would support this, that you should have that capability, but **no military man would propose that** as a means of **conducting a war** which somebody else brought on you to keep them from using nuclear weapons! [Defend/Disputable Assertion]
    Do I make myself clear? [Request for Confirmation]

(15) R: [I believe so.] [Grant/Affirm]

(16) E: It's a fine point in there, you see [Clarification]

(17) R: It's a rather fine distinction. [Cooperative Recycle]

(18) E: Which is why I brought it up in the first place.

(19) R: You're saying that your response is not the mirror image of the enemy's action, but you **have** options short of nuclear war that would do the job. [Cooperative Recycle/Request for Confirmation]

(20) E: **Absolutely! Very well stated**! And **it's a very** different thing. Now, I had nothing to do with the developing this latter thing at all, except for cheering **it on** and helping with these **studies** toward developing the establishment of options. =

R: [uh huh]

E: = I had nothing to do with the other, but it is a thing that's frequently lost sight of, and it's a fine point which is why I wanted to make it. [Grant/Affirm][23]

In the next sample, contradiction unfolds in turns 1–4, although R's vocalic cues appear to be supportive.

(01) R: How did he and Nitze share responsiblity in the ISA? Of course, the responsibility is Nitze's, but he has to do some delegation. How did he split it up with Bundy? [Request for Information]

(02) E: Well, ((uh)) Bundy took on most of the military assistance chores for the ISA I would say. =

R: [uh huh]

E: = For example, later on when we had a new program for India, Bill Bundy headed the group on that. He took on a large bit of the responsibility for Southeast Asia problems and in general if it was Southeast Asia business everybody went to Bill Bundy for it. In other words, he handled some of these things directly for Mr. Nitze. He handled a lot of spade work, the detail work that had to be done to develop positions. He worked with the JCS people very well. =

R: [uh huh]

E: = He had an excellent working relationship all over Washington. [Grant/Assertion]

(03) R: I asked you if he was identified with a particular policy line. Let me ask it a little differently. Any occasion in which you knew that he had come up against a particularly tough opposition on something that he and Nitze and McNamara were really convinced of were pushing? [Request for Information]

(04) E: (9.67) I don't recall anything specific in that line. I know there were differences of opinion, different lines of action proposed, ((uh)) but I don't put these down as, say, ((uh)) being more than you would normally expect to find within different agencies. =

R: [uh huh, uh huh]

E: = I think that in any group you always have different ideas. You **should** have different ideas proposed and worked out and then courses of action decided after good discussion of all factors and opposing viewpoints! =

R: [uh huh]

E: = So I can't give you, say, opposing philosophies particularly. I don't know that we had opposing philosophies? I can't say that Bill Bundy was always in opposition to State, for example, or with JCS. We differed on points as you expect would be normal in any conduct of affairs. (9.54) Perhaps I keep coming back to this point that there were differences, but by and large these differences are ones you **expect** or **want to be brought out**! In other words if you're going to make a difficult decision you should know what the various possibilities are what different courses of action are possible, what do various people recommend we do? if only one course of action is considered you're not really getting a **good background**, a good basis for a decision in all cases. [Refuse/Assertion][24]

As the dialogue continues, the interviewer's ability to challenge the first answer by presenting a disputable assertion appears to facilitate the emergence of hermeneutical conversation. We also see the interviewee's willingness to consider an alternative interpretation of the issue. The speech and counterspeech (including paralinguistic cues) that occur represent the kind of interaction necessary for transcending the performance rules that mitigate against this kind of dialogue.

(05) R: All right, fine. I see this and yet I have had some experience from the **lower** end =

E: [uh huh]

R: = looking up at this, and there's constant pressure to develop an **agency line** on a particular thing so that the agency itself goes united to an interagency meeting. [Mitigated Challenge/Disputable Assertion]

(06) E: This is true. [Admit/Affirm]

(07) R: With a policy position. [Request for Confirmation/ Prompt]

(08) E: Yes. [Grant/Confirm]

(09) R: And again there's an effort to get a united position among all the different agencies' departments, and so on. [Request

for Confirmation/Disputable Assertion]

(10) E: Yes, yes Well, certainly we always tried to work out a **defense** position on any particular problem based on the thinking of say McNamara and a different viewpoint that may have been expressed by the JCS say, didn't surface at an interagency meeting because we always used the Sec. Def. position. [Grant/Affirm]

(11) R: Uh huh. All right. Now, how does the president get the points of view that **have not** been represented in a Sec. Def. position, assuming he needs them? [Request for Clarification]

(12) E: Well, here you have to rely on the fact that in nearly every major decision, there's a representative of the JCS there at the White House meetings, and that they have a chance to air their views if they are in opposition to say a Sec. Def. position. I think there were times when the Secretary **deliberately surfaced** opposing positions! and points of view! so that the President **would** get the benefit of this, although I don't know from my own experience.

R: [uh huh]

E: In other words, he could have said that the JCS have not supported this perhaps he could have I'm speculating now.

R: [uh huh]

E: But I think that there was **always** an **opportunity** for opposing views to be presented.

R: Let me get you to talk about

E: = For example, in interagency meetings with State, I never felt that the JCS representative was in any way (7.7) held down. If we had a meeting with State on a problem, we always tried to see that an ISA and a JCS man were there, so if there were opposing points of view, they **could be brought out!** [Grant/Assertion]

As noted earlier, hermeneutical conversation did not emerge regularly in the interviews examined, a fact that is probably representative of interviews with elite respondents. However, the factors that contribute to the emergence of hermeneutical conversation include the interviewer's use of requests for confirmation, disputable assertions, and mitigated challenges. In addition, third-turn responses to answers as well as supportive vocalic cues by the interviewer play a critical role in the evolution of the challenged record.

Summary

This chapter focuses on the achievement of cooperation and coherence while producing a challenged record. The interviewer's role involves both eliciting and assessing the information provided by the respondent. The rule of admitting disputability of events and the rule of disputable assertions have been discussed within the context of the interviewer's role in producing a challenged record. Two outcomes of a challenged record have been examined. These are the discourse forms of contradiction and hermeneutical conversation. The norm of saving face and the structural constraint of the imagined audience apparently mitigate against the emergence of hermeneutical conversation. Interviewers and interviewees must transcend the rule system to create hermeneutical conversation. Techniques for transcending the rule system depend on verbal and nonverbal cues that can be interpreted as supportive and cooperative in light of structural and substantive disagreement.

4

Storytelling in
Oral History as
Collaborative Production

This chapter is about storytelling in oral history interview conversation. A story is defined as "a specific past-time narrative that makes a point."[1] Just as stories constitute a large portion of casual conversation,[2] so stories constitute large segments of oral history interviews, especially when R's role is neutral elicitor of information. My interest here is in explaining how interviewers and their respondents jointly produce stories for the record. Prior to describing that production process, however, it is necessary to review certain constraints operating in the oral history interview situation. Clearly, these constraints influence the creation and management of stories in the interview situation.

There are *topical* constraints that influence topic selection and management during the interview. Of relevance here is the necessity for interviewees to exert topic control through their answers as contrasted with interviewer's topic control exerted through questions and third-turn responses. Only the interviewee is privileged to tell stories. The interrogator's role, on the other hand, is limited to eliciting stories and to commenting on those stories. We should expect to find respondents utilizing storytelling as a topic control device.

These topical constraints interact with the *goal-related* constraints of the interview situation. The interviewee's goal(s) in the interview influence how stories are managed during the interaction. We should expect to find respondents achieving multiple goals through storytelling. Such goals might include the presentation of a particular self-image and of the role played in the event being discussed.

Likewise, the *procedural* constraints surrounding the interview situation impact on the production of stories. Two important procedural constraints are the norms of coherence and cooperation. The respondent is expected to be coherent in answering the questions. Story production must be managed accordingly; that is, the teller must constantly address the implicit evaluative response of the listener: "So what?" The teller must show that the story is both topical and meaningful—that it makes a point. Generally, the interviewee as storyteller is expected to "(a) tell a topically coherent story; (b) tell a narratable story—one worth building a prolonged telling around; (c) introduce the story so that the connection with previous talk is clear; (d) tell a story that begins at the beginning, that is, one in which time moves ahead reasonably smoothly except for flashbacks that seem to serve a justifiable purpose in the telling; and, (e) evaluate states and events so that it is possible to recover the core of the story and thereby infer the point being made through the telling."[3] As a rule, stories are locally occasioned. "A properly managed storytelling seems to emerge from the ongoing talk—to be occasioned by some point being made in the conversation."[4] A story can be locally occasioned in three different ways: (1) a story can be "triggered" by the content and direction of the ongoing talk; for example the storyteller is "reminded" of a tale "which may or may not be topically coherent with the talk in progress"; (2) a story can be "methodically introduced into turn-by-turn talk";[5] and (3) a story can be requested by the interviewer.

Cooperation between interviewer and interviewee in story production is also required. The interviewer as story recipient is expected to "(a) agree to hear a story if it is proposed or present a reason why it should not be told; (b) agree to hear a story if requested; (c) refrain from taking a turn except to make remarks demonstrating that the story is being followed and understood or asking questions that relate directly to what is being told about the storyworld; and, (d) at the end of the telling, demonstrate understanding by making comments demonstrating that the point of the story has been understood."[6]

Finally, the *structural* constraint of the imagined audience influences story production. We should expect to find the teller weaving a narrative for the benefit of both the interviewer and the imagined audience. Techniques for addressing both audiences relative to the topical, goal-related, and procedural constraints are displayed in the discourse itself.

In order to describe this complex activity of storytelling in turn-by-turn interview talk, it is necessary to introduce a lengthy excerpt from an interview with a journalist who covered the 1960 presidential campaign of John F. Kennedy.[7]

1	(01) R:	((uh)) Could you detail for us the conversation you had
2		with him when you flew uh to West Virginia?
3	(02) E:	Yeah, that is an interesting conversation. I was the only
4		reporter aboard the "Caroline," and I'd asked if it were possible
5		for me to go down and the others were already in West Virginia so
6		I went down. He had a scratchy throat, and he didn't want to
7		talk
8		so we didn't have much of a conversation. He sat in the back. I
9		sat up front. I didn't want to intrude on him, but I did go back
10		and tell him that I had been born and raised in the area of West
11		Virginia that we were going to, the southern West Virginia. We
12		were going to the county seat of the county in which I was born
13		and raised, McDowell County. The county seat was Welch. He had
14		a rally in Welch, and we were going there, and then we were going

15	to drive up through this valley in which I had lived! I told him
16	this, and he was quite fascinated by the idea that I was a West
17	Virginian ((and uh)) I hadn't been back in about twenty years,
18	twenty-five years. This was going to be my first trip back
19	there. Maybe it was even thirty years because I was a young boy
20	when I left there. But the conversation going down was not
21	desultory. I explained this to him, and that was the size of it.
22	He was angry when we got to, the plane landed, We didn't land in
23	Welch, I don't believe. We landed somewhere else and drove to
24	Welch. But he was a little annoyed at an AP
25	reporter—Associated Press reporter—whose name was Arthur
26	Edson, who was covering the campaign, because Arthur Edson had
27	written that his voice, which he didn't want to use when he was
28	around talking to reporters or in close quarters, seemed suddenly
29	to miraculously improve when he got amongst crowds. He thought
30	this was an unfair story. He didn't know Arthur Edson, so when
31	we landed, he said, "Who's Arthur Edson?" I said, "Well, he's an
32	Associated Press reporter, a very good, fair man." Well, he told
33	me about these stories. I had seen one of them. He wanted me to
34	point Arthur Edson out to him and I didn't see him at the airport
35	Well, anyhow we went through this Welch rally. I met some people
36	there that I had known or who had known my father or my brother,
37	older brother and I talked to them about the campaign, and I
38	talked to one, a man named Judge Sid Christie who was a

39   Democratic power in that county and Sid Christie and his brother

40   Sam Christie were from my little town. In fact his brother was

41   my father's lawyer 40 years, years, years ago. My father died in

42   1928 so you can see how far back that went and I was very young

43   of course. But Christie

44   told me that he was going to win in McDowell County. The young

45   man who is postmaster in the town that I lived in had just come

46   from a postmaster's convention in Clarksburg, West Virginia, and

47   he was so excited about the prospect that Kennedy was going to

48   win in West Virginia and he told me he was going to win flat!

49   Oh, I shrugged it off. I thought his was the enthusiasm of a

50   rally, and they're Democrats, and they were kind of partial to

51   Kennedy over Humphrey for reasons which I didn't understand

52   because Humphrey was a poor boy who a West Virginian would kind

53   of appreciate! Anyhow, we went through the valley and up to

54   White Sulpher Springs, I think it was where we got on the plane

55   to come back to Washington. Again, I'm the only reporter. I

56   think there may have been one other reporter aboard now, but I'm

57   not sure. I think I still was the only one. I wish I'd saved

58   the postcard because he wrote on a postcard and had the girl, the

59   stewardess aboard the plane, bring it up to me. He says, "Pete,

60   how do you see the race?" signed Jack. That's one of the reasons

61   I wish I had saved the postcard, but I lost it. I never realized

62   it was a postcard written by a president-to-be, I guess. In any

63   case, I went back, and I remember kneeling at his seat in this

64   little plane of his and saying, "I tell you, I think you're going

65   to win in West Virginia, but I think also that you're going to

66   win big." He looked at me kind of funny and said, "Oh, you've

67   been talking to Sid Christie!" I said, "Yes, I have, and I've

68   been talking to others." Sid Christie was a kind of boss, you

69   see, and Kennedy knew he was all for him. As a matter of fact,

70   Kennedy went to Sid Christie earlier—Christie told me in a later

71   meeting I had with Christie—and asked him whether as a Catholic

72   he ought to enter the West Virginia primary. Christie told me

73   that Kennedy had called him from Phoenix, Arizona and told him he

74   wanted to see him and met him in the lobby of a hotel, I think,

75   in Charleston, West Virginia, put the question to him very

76   straight, "Can I, as a Catholic, enter this race and have a

77   chance of winning it?" and Christie told him a story which I

78   think

79   is interesting. I think Christie's still alive, and perhaps

80   you'll put him on tape and you'll get a more accurate account of

81   this. Christie says that if he as a young man had uh gone to

82   his parents and said he was going to marry a Catholic girl, they

83   would have been horrified and scandalized. He says, "On the

84   other hand, if my daughter came to me and said I'm going to marry

85   a Catholic boy, I wouldn't think twice about it. That's how much

86   of a change has occurred in this state!" But to get back to the

87   plane again, I told Kennedy that it's true I had talked to

88   Christie, but I also had talked to other people! I further told

89   him that if McDowell County was going to go for him in a big way,

90   I saw no reason why the adjacent counties, Mingo County and Logan

91   County—I remembered them from my boyhood—all of which are coal

92   mining counties and the people are no different—bigotry didn't

93   stop at a county line or didn't begin at a county line—I said if

94   there was so little bigotry that McDowell would vote for him, I

95   was sure he was going to win Logan and Mingo counties. Well, he

96   looked thoughtfully about this, but we didn't say much more about

97   it. There's a sequel to this story of great interest that maybe

98   I ought to tell at this point.

99   (03) R: Yes.

100   (04) E: Let me do it. ((uh)) When he was nominated in Los

101   Angeles, we all got aboard a plane to fly to Hyannis Port and I

102   was aboard the plane before he was so, contrary to what some of

103   my colleagues

104   thought, I didn't arrange the seat behind him! I was seated

105   there when he moved in with Toby McDonald, his friend, and sat

106   in front of me. So I had kind of a long interview with him, or

107   discussion, over the back of the plane seat in fact between the

108   crack of the plane seat, you know, the front seat. I said to

109   him, "When did you uh first know that you were over the

110   hump?" My

111   question really was directed at the convention! but he thought I

112   meant when during the campaign? and he said, of course, "After

113   West

114   Virginia. I thought then I was going to make it! And he says

115   and by the way,

116   you were one of the few reporters who told me that I was going

117   to make it! see." And I said, "Yes, and I want to tell you a

118	sad story about that! When I got back to Washington, the
119	*Editor and Publisher* representative in Washington came to me
120	and said, "You've been to West Virginia. Who do you think is
121	going to win?" I said, "Kennedy's going to win. I think he's
122	going to win hands down." The reporter was Pat Munroe. The
123	*Editor and Publisher* reporter was Pat Munroe who knew Kennedy.
124	and he called me up a day or so later, and he said, "Say, I've
125	been
126	talking to some other people who've been in West Virginia, and
127	they say you'd better stick to diplomatic affairs and foreign
128	affairs. But I wondered if I could quote you?" I said, "Well,
129	most especially now you can quote me since they think I don't
130	know anything about politics." So he did quote me as saying
131	Kennedy was going to win. My editor in Chicago saw this quote
132	and said, "Hooray! Good! This was after he won. Let's get out
133	what Pete wrote about West Virginia, and let's make a pro-motion
134	ad about it!" We had the front page of *Editor and Publisher*
135	on alternate issues with a *Chicago Daily News* ad. So they got
136	my copy from West Virginia. I think I only wrote two stories
137	because I was only down there for eight hours or so on that
138	trip. And they couldn't find a line in which I had predicted
139	that Kennedy was going to win in West Virginia! They called me
140	up and said, "Didn't you ever write this?" "Of course not, I
141	didn't write it. I'm in the business for some time. I'm not
142	going to do what the *Literary Digest* did in 1936! I'm not in
143	the business of prophecy! This was a conversation." I told
144	Kennedy this. Well anyhow, my boss was very unhappy about
145	this, and I told ((uh)) Kennedy the story and he was amused by
146	it.
147	He said, "It reminds me of an experience I had as a reporter!"

148   He worked for Hearst briefly, for International News
149   Service. They sent him to England in 1945. "The reason
150   this story's vivid in my mind is that I was in England at the
151   time. I spent eighteen months in England during the war
       and
152   I came back in '45. I was in Paris when I came back, but I
153   knew about the British election campaign. Well anyhow,
       And I
154   predicted that
155   Atlee was going to win! the Labour party is going to win,
       because
156   all of the working people I talked to thought, "Well, Chur-
       chill
157   was a great war time prime minister, but now that war is
158   won, it's time to turn him out to pasture!" So Kennedy told
       me
159   that he had gotten to London and talked to some people and
       sat
160   down and wrote a story that Labour was going to win this
161   election and the Hearst people were furious
162   about this young reporter over there reporting that the Brit-
       ish
163   were going to turn out the war time hero! and they sent him
       a
164   long cable and he said he spent days kind of getting off of
165   that
166   limb and finally, he worked it around to where Churchill's
167   Conservative Party strength had rallied! and Churchill now
       was
168   going to win. See, just shortly before the election, he had it
169   all straightened out. Of course, the election came and Labour
170   won. If he'd stuck with his original position, he would have
171   been a hero but he said to me, "I didn't, and I was like a lot
172   of other reporters wrong." So he was trying to make me feel
       a
173   little better about this episode of West Virginia. And I'm
174   sorry I didn't write the story out of West Virginia because
       I
175   would have been in a minority. Later on there were people
       who
176   said they, too, had predicted that he would win in West
177   Virginia, but at least I had his word for it that he thought I
178   was one of the few reporters that had told him this. It was

179   only because I had met these people who had known my
        parents and
180   who had told me he was going to win. Eight hours. I had no
181   time to make an independent judgment.

The obvious place to begin this analysis is with the emergence of stories. Stories are introduced by the respondent into interview discourse in two ways. They can be triggered by a prior answer (e.g., "That reminds me . . .") and they can be methodically introduced into the talk. Stories also can be requested by the interviewer. All of these instances require "entrance talk" on the part of the storyteller. In addition, stories serve various functions in the negotiated conversation. In other words, interviewers do not necessarily request stories as a part of the questioning process. Instead their questions (requests for information) serve as potential entry points for stories. The stories can be used as answers, explanations, accounts, justifications, clarifications, warnings, prophecies, etc.

The above excerpt contains illustrations of two introductory devices as well as the accompanying entrance talk. For example, the first story is made possible by the interviewer's request, "Could you detail for us the conversation you had with him when you flew to West Virginia?" Here, the rule of request for information discussed in chapter 2 is in operation. E's entrance talk signals compliance with the request, "Yes, that is an interesting conversation," and the story begins. At the end of turn 02, E methodically introduces another story (lines 97–98) saying, "There's a sequel to this story of great interest that maybe I ought to tell at this point." This entrance talk functions as a request for permission to provide information (see the rule of indirect request for permission to provide information in chapter 2) that is granted by R's "Yes," (line 99). These turns illustrate both that storytelling is recipient designed and that the privilege of telling a story is a negotiated outcome between interviewer and interviewee. Bracketing moves, which were discussed earlier, such as techniques for organizing talk, are used frequently in stories. Such devices allow the teller to comment on his or her own talk. When this happens the storyteller takes on a role much like that of a narrator in a play or that of the chorus in a Greek tragedy. So, many levels of interaction occur simultaneously in the storytelling. Note also that the entrance talk/request occurs at the end of E's first turn at speaking. Thus the entrance talk serves as a means for maintaining the floor, for controlling the topic flow, and for displaying cooperation within the procedural norms of the interview as a communicative event. The use of this device at this juncture in the interview is particularly interesting due to the lengthy turn (02) by E. The overall effect is of E dominating the interaction, even though one can assume that R is providing positive nonverbal feedback to E.

Having shown how entrance talk as an illocutionary act can function as a topic management device, the analytical focus can shift to the story itself and to the implicit negotiation process occurring in four turns at talk. One feature of that implicit negotiation process is that the storyteller designed the story for its recipients. The question posed here is: How does the teller design the story for the recipients—the interviewer and the imagined audience? In other words, E is expected to be cooperative in the interview by telling a story that can be heard by R and the imagined audience as topical, relevant, meaningful, interesting, etc. Hence the story itself should display interpretive markers that identify the story's structure and function.

Here we see that the rule of request for information and the rule of narrative response are operable as turn 02 begins. The rule of narrative response says: "If A makes a request for information to B, and B immediately begins a narrative, then B is heard as asserting that the evaluative point of the narrative will supply the information requested."[8] Furthermore, R is able to recognize that a narrative is beginning because of the entrance talk by E that confirms that the conversation mentioned by R is worth telling. The next statement, "I was the only reporter aboard the 'Caroline,' and I'd asked if it were possible for me to go down," signals the beginning of the story. The statement introduces the story's orientation—one of the classic structural units of narrative.[9] Of course, functionally the orientation provides relevant background for understanding the story. For example, the orientation makes reference to situational characteristics such as time, place, actors, and actions that are pertinent to the story. Here the rule of narrative orientation enables the listener to interpret the statement "I was the only reporter aboard the 'Caroline' . . , as an orienting sentence rather than as the response itself. The key is that the statement "is not reportable in itself."[10] Hence the statement is heard as a reference to the response that will follow and can be interpreted within the framework of the rule of narrative orientation: "If A makes reference to an event that occurred prior to the time of speaking, which cannot be interpreted by any rule of discourse as a complete speech action in itself, then B will hear this reference as the orientation to a narrative to follow."[11]

To this point, we see that teller and listener are collaborating in the production of the story even though the listener's collaboration is primarily nonverbal in nature. Their collaboration is dependent upon their taken-for-granted knowledge of certain interpretive rules and performance rules that govern the oral history interview as a communicative event. The development of the story also depends upon negotiation of such rule-based knowledge.

Returning to the story (turn 02), we see that the orientation is rather lengthy and complex. Lines 3–30 provide contextual details about the reason for the trip and the seating arrangement of the principal actors. All of this talk can be heard as preliminary to the actual response to the question. The statement "But the conversation going down was not desultory" (lines 20–21) signals that E has not made his evaluative point; the point can be made by extending the temporal frame beyond the plane ride to West Virginia.

At this point, E digresses into a report of a brief conversation with Kennedy (lines 24–34). Technically, this report can be construed as an answer to the question of turn 01. I contend, however, that E realizes that the response is not satisfactory because E earlier established the expectation that he would present a story as his response. E appears to be searching for that story as he talks. I believe this exemplifies the creative processes involved in interview communication. In other words, aware of his obligation to provide a cooperative and coherent narrative response, the respondent talks his way to that narrative. With the statement "Well, anyhow we went through this Welch rally" (line 35), we see the orientation to the first storyline, which begins with E identifying principal actors and initial actions in the unfolding narrative. The phrase "well anyhow" recurs through E's lengthy turns. In North American culture, "well anyhow" functions to retrieve an original theme or storyline and to repair the teller's flirtation with nonrelevance. In other words, tellers monitor their talk and use bracketing devices such as "well anyhow" to direct their own talk (and to keep control of the floor). In these instances, "well anyhow" is equivalent to saying, "well, to get back to the point of this story."

The next segment of talk illustrates another interesting feature of collaborative story production. I refer to the process by which the teller makes the background (what might be regarded as digressions) information pertinent to the listener and to the storyline. As the story begins to unfold, in line 36 E identifies important characters whereupon E inserts background information about his own childhood. While this information could be excluded without damaging the storyline, the inclusion of the information is heard as pertinent. E is allowed the privilege to insert such material as a part of the overall privilege that is legitimized through the role of storyteller. Apparently, speakers and listeners establish tolerance thresholds for extraneous information. One might suggest that the teller tests those waters through trial and error. Hence R and E jointly establish their own parameters for relevance and coherence. Again, I assume that R's collaboration is primarily nonverbal and supportive.

As the action unfolds, the temporal sequence of events is depicted through the use of narrative clauses that have past tense forms and present tense forms as their main verbs. For example, E develops the storyline as follows:

(35) "I met some people . . . "
(37) "I talked to them . . . "
(37–38) "I talked to one . . . "
(43–44) "Christie told me . . . "
(48) " . . . he told me . . . "
(49) "Oh, I shrugged it off . . ."
(53) "Anyhow, we went through the valley . . . "

(55) "Again, I'm the only reporter . . . "
(57–58) "I wish I'd saved the postcard . . . "
(59–60) "He says, 'Pete, how do you see the race,' signed Jack."
(62–64) "In any case, I went back and I remember kneeling at his seat in this little
(64–65) plane of his and saying, 'I tell you, I think you're going to win in West Virginia . . . "
(66–67) "He looked at me . . . and said, 'Oh, you've been talking to Sid Christie!' I said, 'Yes' . . . "

The rule of narrative sequencing enables the listener to interpret the above sequence of past tense verbs and present tense verbs as being an accurate recounting of the chronology of events: "In a narrative, if A refers to an event with a sentence S_1 that has a nonstative main verb in the preterit or present tense, and then refers to another event with a sentence S_2 of the same structure, then B will hear A as asserting that the event referred to by S_1 took place before the event referred to by S_2."[12]

As the story continues, the structure becomes more complex as the first embedded story is told (lines 69–86). Clearly, this story is not to be construed as occurring in the sequence of events under discussion. Rather, the story should be heard as functioning to illuminate the temper of the times in West Virginia as well as the relationship between Kennedy and Christie, a local political boss. The discourse is especially interesting because E also tells another embedded story that is attributed to Christie. So several storylines are being managed at this juncture in turn 02. Moreover, we see that the teller is adroit at suspending the forward movement of the narrative (lines 69–86). He also achieves the suspension through his intonation and through his insertion of an explanation to the listener: "Sid Christie was a kind of boss, you see," an aside that stands outside the storyline itself. Utterances such as "As a matter of fact" function as entrance talk for a forthcoming embedded story. Such a technique can also function to build suspense for the listener. It appears that the embedded stories serve as markers for the evaluation—another structural characteristic of narratives. The action and the forthcoming point of the entire story are delayed while the teller adds information that can heighten listener interest in the drama. This ability to weave stories filled with vivid details about main and supporting actors, external but related actions, and digressions that suspend the main action appears to distinguish superior storytellers from mediocre ones. It also appears that listeners are willing to give tellers a chance to demonstrate their storytelling abilities. So if the teller can accomplish a cooperative, suspenseful, coherent telling, then the listener is willing to wait for the point of the story to be made.

In this story, the point is finally made as the teller returns to the original storyline. Again, the teller underscores his account of telling Kennedy that he would win big in West Virginia. The story is concluded—the coda—when Kennedy's response is recounted (lines 96–97). The coda functions to bring the listener back into the present time and signals to the listener that a particular story is over. At this point, R methodically introduces another story into the interview saying, "There's a sequel to this story of great interest that maybe I ought to tell at this point." R grants this request to tell another story, and the orientation to the new story begins (lines 100–108).

This time the orientation is shorter, but it serves the function of setting the stage for the upcoming narrative which begins on line 109. This narrative is followed by the first embedded story within this turn. Here E recollects a story told to him by Kennedy (lines 147–72). In fact, he justifies inclusion of the story by saying, "The reason this story's vivid in my mind. . . . " Such discourse signals that E is obligated to make the embedded story relevant for the listener and pertinent to the general storyline. At the conclusion of this talk, the teller's evaluation or point of the story begins to emerge (lines 173–81). In fact, it is the first evaluation of this lengthy episode that signals that this story, which includes all of the embedded stories, is about to end.

To this point, storytelling has been shown to be a complex, collaborative activity that when carried out competently can be used to maintain the floor, to control the topics, and to make points. Another goal of the teller may be to establish a self-image relative to the events being recounted. The story sequel (turn 04) is of interest because of its contrast with the earlier stories told in turn 02; that is, by turn 04 the teller has shifted the central storyline from Kennedy to himself. The stories that are developed in the sequel serve to establish the teller's image as well as his role in predicting a Kennedy victory. For example, as E recounts his conversation with Kennedy, he tells a story that centers on his experiences as a reporter (lines 109–46). Even the second story attributed to Kennedy is about Kennedy's experience as a reporter rather than about Kennedy's campaign for the presidency (lines 147–72). The point of the first story is made at the end of turn 04: " . . . but at least I had his word for it that he thought I was one of the few reporters that had told him this." Hence turn 04 is utilized by E to establish his own self-image. The turn itself does not shed light on the Kennedy campaign, although one might argue that the information in turn 04 sheds light on Kennedy the man. Such topic management and image management practices constitute the creative processes of oral history interviewing. Clearly, storytelling is a communicative act that allows the informant great flexibility and freedom to control the interview and to maintain coherence and cooperation while doing so. As such we see how storytelling is of pragmatic value for the oral history informant.

Summary

At the beginning of this chapter, I characterized storytelling as a collaborative production between interviewer and interviewee. Analysis of the excerpt from an interview demonstrates the active role played by the teller (the interviewee). I have shown that the teller works constantly to satisfy the constraints necessary for producing coherent, cooperative interaction. Less analytical emphasis is given to the copresent recipient of the story (the interviewer) because his role in achieving coherence and cooperation is executed primarily nonverbally. Absence of access to the visual cues occurring during the interaction, therefore, makes extended discussion of the recipient's role in storytelling impossible. Absence of evidence to the contrary, I have assumed that this production was accomplished smoothly and that the teller received appropriate feedback. In that same vein, I expect that nonverbal cues such as head nods were used in place of comments demonstrating that the story was understood (a conventional reception technique of story recipients). The interviewer does not use his next turn at talk to comment on the stories. The absence of such commentary ordinarily can be construed as a rule violation. Because no evidence of acknowledgment of a rule violation can be found in the discourse, I assume nonverbal cues were used to substitute for the commentary. Such an occurrence appears to be common among the interviews examined in this study. Future investigations of collaborative story production should focus on such issues. Finally, storytelling has been shown to fulfill two functions in interview interaction: a propositional function of talking about a lived-through experience, and a pragmatic function of accomplishing speech actions such as granting requests for information. Understanding both functions is necessary in order to illuminate the interactive processes that constitute oral history conversation.

Communication-Related Issues for Oral Historians

Throughout this book, I emphasize the interactive nature of the oral history interview by demonstrating the principles of interpretation and communicative performance that constitute oral interviews with elite respondents. Special attention is given to those principles that account for achieving cooperation and coherence during interview discourse.

At this time, it is appropriate to turn to a more general discussion of the oral history interview as a communicative event. One goal in this chapter is to paint a picture of the human communication processes that underlie the activity of oral history interviewing. A second goal is to explore certain communication-related issues pertaining to the practice of oral history that are derived from the theoretical grounding and descriptive analyses contained in this book. Any excursion into that domain requires a discussion of central conceptions about human communication, the vehicle for the creation of the oral interview.

A STATE OF INTERSUBJECTIVITY IS A PRECONDITION FOR HUMAN SYMBOL-USING ACTIVITY. As we know it, symbolic interaction functions by virtue of the tacit assumption of the existence of an intersubjective world, a world constituted by shared perceptions and commonsense knowledge about everyday life. The world "is intersubjective because we live in it as men among other men, bound to them through common influence and work, understanding others and being understood by them. It is a world of culture because, from the outset, the world of everyday life is a universe of significance to us, that is, a texture of meaning which we have to interpret in order to find our bearings within it and come to terms with it."[1] In order to understand how human communication takes place, the "here-and-now" of commonsense knowledge "has to be conceived of as an intersubjectively established social reality."[2] In other words, some commonality or common ground must exist in order to move toward even a partial synchronization of symbols and their meanings. This commonality serves to bridge the differences between individualized perspectives, thus creating the grounds for various forms of communication, for example, conversation, interviews, public speech, group discussion, and their outcomes (e.g., negotiation, information gathering, problem solving, and compromise). It is this intersubjectively known world that allows individuals to place order on the "booming, buzzing" social world. But what are the origins of this commonality? The bridge of commonality provided by commonsense thinking results from certain taken-for-granted idealizations about human existence that, in turn, originate from and are perpetuated through practice.

One of those idealizations—reciprocity of perspectives—means that although individuals are aware of their inherent differences as individuals, generally they ignore those differences in everyday life by assuming the existence of reciprocal orientations toward practical life.[3] You see the world as I do and vice versa. One aspect of that reciprocal orientation involves a similarity in selective perception:

Until counterevidence I take it for granted—and assume my fellow-man does the same—that the differences in perspectives originating in our unique biographical situations are irrelevant for the purpose at hand of either of us and that he and I, that "We" assume that both of us have selected and interpreted the actually or potentially common objects and their features in an identical manner or at least an "empirically identical" manner, i.e., one sufficient for all practical purposes.[4]

These "common objects," of course, are manifested in the occurrences of everyday life and take myriad forms, such as, codes, customs, beliefs, linguistic devices, folkways, traditional behavior, laws, etc. As such, they constitute and are constituted by the social world. In fact, much of the common knowledge that an individual takes for granted is derivative; that is, it is transmitted through linguistic codes.[5]

On the other hand, we recognize that knowledge about the world is "socially distributed" in terms of cultures, training, experience, biography, and so on. Commonsense knowledge takes this social distribution into account, enabling social actors to make distinctions about each other and about their social worlds. The depiction of the intersubjective world, therefore, is one of assumed commonality (reinforced through practice) juxtaposed with individuality. These elements coexist in a relationship of tension in everyday life.

Because of this tension-laden relationship, I chose American male elites as the starting point for my inquiry. Presumably, the differences between American male elite informants and American male elite interviewers are outweighed by their commonalities. Clearly, the differences begin to outweigh the similarities when one thinks about the kinds of interviewer/ interviewee relationships found in oral history; differences arise out of social relationships defined by class, age, gender, race, ethnic origin, and socioeconomic status, to name a few.

Given this tension-laden, intersubjective world, certain commonsense knowledge must be presumed in order to engage in the interview process. Given the fact that absolute commensurability of perspectives is impossible, "some commonality is . . . established by the very fact that two persons engage in a dialogue."[6] There is a commonality of experience evidenced by the participation of the two parties in a common event in the "here-and-now"; that is, the oral historian and the respondent experience the interview event together. This situation, in turn, presupposes other taken-for-granted features of commonality. These include the fact that the parties assume a "we" relationship that is complementary by virtue of the necessity for alternating roles as speaker and listener. For example, in the oral history interview those roles are constrained by the fact that the historian serves as the interrogator while the other party is the respondent. Furthermore, this complementary relationship between speaker and listener presupposes a substantial amount of shared, usually tacit, knowledge about the practical accomplishment of conversation. The expansive repertoire of knowledge about requesting information, refusing requests, challenging intepretations, managing topics, etc. possessed by interviewers and interviewees is demonstrated throughout this book. The interactants also display extensive understanding of prescriptions about the proper communicative attitude such as cooperation, conciseness, relevance, and politeness. The point is that all of this taken-for-granted knowledge must be present in order for an oral history interview to be accomplished. This knowledge is layered upon a foundation of intersubjective knowledge about the nature of social reality, and of course, this knowledge is culturally bounded. Grice's cooperative principle and Brown and Levinson's notion about politeness and "face" must be understood culturally. It remains to be seen how pertinent such ideas are in various oral history contexts. Finally, certain interpersonal abilities of the individual actors must be present in order for an interview to be enacted. It is necessary to have the ability to take the perspective of the other, meaning that individual A is able to see himself or herself as an object in the eyes of individual B. These abilities are manifested in the interviews as recipient-designed talk. In these oral history interviews, the talk was designed for both the interviewer and the imagined audience. The sequence of stories examined in chapter 4 is particularly revealing of the informant's ability to design stories for recipients. For example, the teller demonstrated the topical relevance of a story not only by reference to its locally occasioned occurrence but also by reference to its projected reception by the interviewer. Likewise, the creation of unchallenged records and challenged records by the interviewer can be construed as being designed for imagined audiences. Perspective-taking, therefore, is a prerequisite for communicative competence across situations. A state of intersubjectivity is a precondition for human symbol-using activity and for communicative competence. This state is assumed to underlie the discussion of the remainder of the conceptions about human communication.

HUMAN COMMUNICATION IS A CREATIVE PROCESS THROUGH WHICH SOCIAL (INTERSUBJECTIVE) REALITY IS CONSTRUCTED. Not only is intersubjectivity necessary in order to communicate, but it is also generated through the act of communicating. The world that is created through communication is comprised primarily of social facts—agreements about the nature of social activity and what behaviors count as facts.[7]

It is through the process of human communication that social facts are created, sustained, changed, repaired, and shared. As Delia and Grossberg note, "communication is an emergent, creative activity through which human social reality is constantly being recreated, affirmed, repaired, and changed."[8]

From this viewpoint, human behavior is cognitively grounded and self-reflexive. One way to depict such activity is by viewing humans as improvisational actors on the stage of everyday life. These actors exist in an actional, not a mechanistic, life-world in which activity and meaning are constructed, not released. The meaning construction process emerges out of interaction—the joining of two or more lines of behavior—that is bound up in verbal and nonverbal symbols.[9] The meaning that emerges in any given context is dependent upon the interplay between the individual and the social; that is, the meaning of social objects depends upon the meanings that one's in-group gives to them and upon the interpretive processes of the individual. Each individual's remembrance of the past, understanding of the present, and anticipation of the future influence the construction of meaning. These individual and social factors interact in the production of meaning. Furthermore, one's account of a lived-through experience is retrospective in nature in that it is through reflection that one's lived-experience acquires its meaning. "Meaning is not a quality inherent in certain experiences emerging within our stream of consciousness but the result of an interpretation of a past experience looked at from the present Now with a reflective attitude."[10] Even so, this reflective meaning is tested against the understandings of others in order to arrive at an acceptable or intersubjective meaning of reality. Throughout this book, we have seen how the oral interview is a vehicle used to prompt reflective meanings of lived-through experiences. For example, the question "((uh)) Could you detail for us the conversation you had with him when you flew ((uh)) to West Virginia?" enables the respondent to share memories of his experiences during the 1960 presidential campaign. In fact, what we receive is a montage of recollections that bears more or less on the initial question. We also have seen how the interviewer's role (as elicitor of information versus as elicitor and assessor of information) influences greatly the interpretation of lived-through experience that becomes inscribed as a historical record. For example, the examination of ideas and the expansion of themes during interaction is much greater in challenged records. One kind of record is not necessarily more valuable than the other. But the records are notably different, and the difference is produced by the interviewer communication strategies and the interpretation and negotiation with the interviewee.

Human communication, therefore, is the process by which humans symbolically coordinate their respective worldviews. The coordination process involves the negotiation of situated definitions. This coordination, or negotiation, process focuses on the communicative intentions of the interactants. "In communication," O'Keefe and Delia explain,

action is mobilized to serve the needs of expression and interpretation is guided by attribution of the intention to express. Thus, although many different intentions direct communicative action (e.g., to persuade or to soothe distressed feelings), at base communication originates in the attempt to make publicly available some private state and the organization of behavior toward that end.[11]

Hence human communication is "a process of interaction in which the communicative intentions of participants are a focus of coordination."[12] The product of that process is a socially constructed reality that "in normal discourse is always a partial rather than a complete shared understanding."[13]

[P]urely private experience is transformed into intersubjectively established knowledge by the very act of communication. The speaker's "experiential reality" will in such a case never be made known to the listener as such, in its initial pre-verbal richness and complexity. Which aspects can be made known are partly dependent upon pre-established commonality between the two participants in the dialogue with respect to interpretation, strategies of attribution and cognitive categorization.[14]

This presupposed commonality is referred to as "the reciprocity of motives," implying that "the motives imputed to the Other are typically the same as my own or that of others in typically similar circumstances."[15] The "intersubjectively established here-and-now" of the interaction is what constitutes the situation out of which the communication as coordination of intentions takes place.

As a coordination process, human communication is pervasive in the construction of social reality.

Social creations ranging from a person's self-concept, through relationships we establish with others, to larger social communities, including small groups, organizations, subcultures, and entire cultures, are created by the process of people talking with one another. For instance, people's self perceptions, including feelings of self-worth, are functions of others' positive and negative communicative reactions. Similarly, we establish and maintain relationships, including friendships and romantic partnerships, by talking with others about our common interests. Likewise, groups ranging from small social clubs to nation-states are bound together by mutual needs identified through the process of communication. In this sense, all soccial contracts are created, maintained, and destroyed largely by talk.[16]

From this viewpoint, communication in the oral history interview involves more than mere message exchange through some shared code. Rather, the interview is considered as a situated encounter, founded on a reciprocity of perspectives and motives. In the encounter two parties jointly create an intersubjective reality through a process of anticipatory encoding and decoding. This, in turn, is based upon the coordination, and often the negotiation, of each individual's communicative intentions and meanings. Through this process, meaning is constructed, repaired, changed, and shared.

This interactive process serves as the vehicle for creation of the oral text as historical record. In other words, through the oral interview process a personal lived-through experience is transformed into a public, historical record. It is because of the complexity of the communication process as demonstrated in this book that the oral history interview cannot be regarded as a linear chain of antecedent and consequent acts. The process is more appropriately depicted as a circular one that is emergent and creative in nature; that is, the outcome of the interaction, whether it be in the form of stories, contradiction, or contrariety, transcends the original input. There is a "fusion of horizons" that upon being inscribed as the oral text becomes the historical record. "Thus," as Thompson observes, "while method and meaning can be treated as independent themes, they are at bottom inseparable."[17] Clearly, any understanding of that record and of the oral interview is dependent upon one's understanding of the creative, negotiated process through which such a record originates.

HUMAN COMMUNICATION IS A REASON-BASED PROCESS.   Oral history interviewing is a processs most appropriately accounted for by reason-based explanations that are cognitively grounded rather than by the laws-based explanations grounded in mechanistic, causal assumptions. This respect for human volition, coupled with the beliefs that human communicators are capable of choice and self-directed action[18] and that people communicate for reasons,[19] has led communication scholars to reason-based explanations of the communication proccess. Such teleological explanation adheres to the "presuppositions that human beings make and evaluate choices among alternative courses of action and that many of these choices are made on the basis of rules."[20] Hence, in this sense, "rules explain communication behavior by referring to a communicator's goals, intentions, and reasons for communicating."[21] In fact, proponents of this "actional" view suggest that most communication behaviors are a form of action:

People are entities capable of "symbolic action"; to varying degrees they can be addressed, "reasoned with," petitioned, persuaded. "Things" can but move, or be moved. . . . *Action* involves *character,* which involves *choice*; and the *form* of choice attains its perfection in the distinction between Yes and No (between *thou shalt* and *thou shalt not*). Though the concept of sheer "motion" is non-ethical, "action" implies the ethical (the human personality).[22]

Human behavior "involves an agent capable of deliberating and choosing from a variety of courses of action" those actions that best meet the goals and needs of the moment.[23] The concern, therefore, is not what is done to a person by external forces, although it is acknowledged that uncontrollable phenomena such as intelligence influence communicative choices; rather, the focus is on the "goal-action linkages" made by persons interacting in various situations within an orderly (not random) world. This is to suggest, of course, that reason-based communicative actions are context-dependent, probable in outcome, and grounded in the means-end relationships perceived by the interactants.[24]

Although there are three predominant rules-based explanations currently in use by communication scholars,[25] the explanation grounded in the social actor's intention is pertinent for this discussion of oral history interviewing. The intentional perspective assumes an intersubjective social reality in which people are purposive agents of action who select their lines of action based on a strategic assessment of the goal-action linkages thought to be operative in a given situation. Such a view assumes that the communicators are aware of their goals and of their reasons for their choice of behaviors; it also assumes that others can successfully interpret those linkages and, in fact, that they do. As explained earlier, oral history interview situations are characterized by such explicit goal awareness, in that they reflect situational constraints of moderate to high risk, novelty, and public accessibility. The chapter on storytelling illustrated clearly this goal-awareness relative to the teller and recipients of the stories. Various management devices such as instructing the listener on the importance of the story sequel were used. In a sense, the teller provides an ongoing commentary on the story itself; such commentary is one manifestation of the reason-based communication process.

In addition, this reason-based process is culturally bound.

Everyone takes his or her own culture—the intersubjective reality—for granted. For example, the understanding, or rule, that enables the words "Hi, how do you do?" to function as a greeting rather than as a request for information about one's health with the preferred (prescriptive) response being "Fine, how do you do?" is culturally grounded. Likewise, the rules that underlie the enactment of an interview are understood tacitly by interactants who share a cultural orientation. On the other hand, communication between people of different cultures can be problematic due to the differences in goal-action linkages that can exist. In that case, the interactants may be forced to articulate the operable set of rules before they can interact successfully.

Whatever the case, the oral history interview potentially reflects all of these features, which in turn implies salience of goal-action linkages on the part of the participants. To view communication, therefore, as an intentional or a reason-based process is essential for persons conducting and evaluating oral history interviews.

HUMAN COMMUNICATION TAKES PLACE WITHIN A SOCIO-HISTORICAL CONTEXT. Understanding of communication phenomena cannot be accomplished without consideration of both the synchronic and diachronic features of context. The synchronic elements of context are those variables that constitute the communicative interaction as it happens. These include the social actors, their utterances and nonverbal cues as well as the other extralinguistic factors (such as time, place, occasion, relevant rules, or goal-action relationships), and the operative reciprocal perspectives and motives. Any analysis of communication in the oral history interview, therefore, must be accomplished with the understanding that the social construction of meaning will emerge out of that context.

Similarly, the diachrony of the socio-historical context characterizes the human communication process. The individual is born into a world that is already meaningful.[26] Interpretations, customs, codes, and linquistic systems already exist. To further complicate the matter, there is often more than one cultural perspective for any social situation. A part of the socialization process involves learning to deal with this intersubjective reality. The individual, therefore, has to coordinate one's idiosyncratic views with the larger social reality. Furthermore, there will be continual tension between the individual's view and that of the generalized other. As O'Keefe and Delia explain:

one embraces an entire universe of shared meaning and acquires a range of socially and historically constituted vehicles (a common language, shared cultural understandings, typical modes of interpreting expressions and experiences) for interpretation and communication. However, communication always involves individuals with their own personal interpretive perspectives and projects acting in concrete situations. Hence, the polar terms: constraint and creativity, culture and individuality, language and thought.[27]

The socio-historical context is the matrix out of which this tension between the individual and the cultural takes place. To understand the communication process requires that one acknowledge this tension and account for the interplay between the individual and the social in the interpretation of symbolic activities such as the oral history interview. In other words,

Communication involves messages, and messages are always socially meaningful only within some contextually and historically created system of intersubjectively shared understanding. This is not to maintain that messages do not involve informational or formal structures, but that such structures represent further abstractions from their dense meanings as acts within the ongoing process of interpretation. Communication cannot be decontextualized without destroying its originary meaningfulness for the interlocutors.[28]

It is imperative to acknowledge the contextual (synchronic and diachronic) nature of oral interview data and to utilize both oral and written data as records of the interviews because the recording provides the interpretational cues that cannot be found in a purely written record. In fact, the typed transcription of an interview represents only "the cadaver of speech." "An essential part of what is lost in transcription has to do with . . . meta-linguistic operations, i.e., with shifting premises of communication conveyed by, for example, body movement, gesture, facial expressions, and tone of voice."[29] However, the transcription system used here can reflect some of the nuances of interaction, including pause intervals and vocalic cues. These and other synchronic features of context are increasingly coming to the attention of oral historians. For example, Grele notes that "a community of interest in [language and culture] exists among those whose work and practice is dependent upon knowledge of the contextual analysis of the spoken word."[30] Yet, he adds, "There are really no essays in oral history which discuss language in historical interviewing, although the problems and promises are often mentioned."[31] In view of this state of affairs, Grele's "interdisciplinary" solution of "a fieldwork approach which seeks through recorded interviews to preserve spoken conversations capable of being analyzed by the use of a number of disciplinary perspectives"[32] is currently needed and pointed in the right direction. As Charles Joyner cautioned years ago, the oral history interview is a communicative event, a phenomenon that must be dealt with in its own right, not in truncated fashion merely for the sake of convenience.[33]

If, however, the aim is to provide a complete description of the interview context, then the issue of recording the interviews on videotape must be addressed. Despite Grele's caution about the use of videotape in oral history interviewing,[34] theoretically such video recording makes sense. Through videotape, the oral historian is privy to aspects of the synchronic context that have previously been unavailable for scrutiny, especially nonverbal cues such as facial expressions and body movements that occur during periods of silence and when one party is listening. As I suggested in the discussion of storytelling, only when the visual scene is opened for scrutiny can the eloquence of silence and the process of listening begin to be understood. The point is that human interaction takes place in a complex environment in which all of the sensory mechanisms are operative. Preservation of the visual mode of the oral history interview could contribute to enhanced understanding of how historical data are generated because the critical glance of attention would be enlarged. Methodological and interpretational issues involved with video recording oral history interviews are discussed later in this chapter.

HUMAN COMMUNICATION IS AN OPEN SYSTEM THAT IS DEVELOPMEN-
TAL IN NATURE. Two seminal ideas are pertinent to this assumption about human communication as a process. These
are the corollary notions that such a process is open and developmental.

The conception of openness derives from general systems
philosophy[35] and is a direct refutation of the atomistic, re-
ductionist views of process reflected by the positivist treat-
ments of communication. There are four properties of open
systems that are helpful in understanding the nature of the
interview as an open system: wholeness, synergy, circularity,
and equifinality.

Applying the principle of "nonsummativity" to the interview means that the whole is greater than the sum of its
parts. Watzlawick, Beavin and Jackson underscore this point,
saying, "A system cannot be taken for the sum of its parts;
indeed, formal analysis of artificially isolated segments would
destroy the very object of interest. It is necessary to neglect
the parts for the gestalt."[36] Moreover, there exists a synergistic
relationship among the parts that contributes to the creative
potential of the system. Hence the outcome of dyadic interaction—as in the oral history interview—over time can never
be equated with a simple combination of the communicative
acts as they occurred. Experience shows that mastering a particular technique of questioning will not guarantee a particular
answer; this is so because the outcome of the interaction between interviewer and interviewee is emergent and transcends
the discrete communicative acts of the process. Smith explains: "Each part of a communication system affects every
other part, and the whole of a communication episode is something far greater than the sum of the individual speech acts
constituting it."[37] Understanding this complex process, therefore, cannot involve the analysis of discrete variables. Here
again, the point about treating oral data as if they were written
data becomes relevant. To consider the written transcript to
be representative of the whole communicative event is to vio-
late the fundamental complexity of the communication process itself. The whole is greater than the sum of its parts; the
entirety of the oral history interview must be accounted for
in order for valid conclusions to be drawn.

The special whole-part relationship implied by "wholeness" and "synergy" leads to the corollary property of circularity. Circularity, as contrasted with linearity of the positivist tradition, suggests a reciprocity of influence on the part of the interactants in the interview situation. It also implies a complementarity of roles whereby both parties act as speaker and listener through a series of episodes. The totality of the episodic experiences provides clues to the construction of meaning that occurs in the interview, not in terms of a sequence of cause-effect (antecedent-consequent) chains, but in terms of transformations of meanings that emerge from the reciprocal interaction. The principles of coherence and cooperativity discussed throughout this book are illustrative. Coherence and cooperation make sense only when viewed within the perspective of circularity and wholeness. Coherence, for example, is an overarching concept that is constituted of local, global, and themal coherence; that is, coherent talk is built out of layers of utterances as well as their understandings-interpretations-meanings. All of this is contextually grounded, hence the coherence derives in part from the light in which the talk is seen. Related to the ideas of wholeness and circularity—reciprocal influence—is the property of equifinality.

Equifinality refers to the idea that in an open system, the same goal can be reached in different ways from different starting points. Variations of conversational episodes can move the interactants toward the achievement of the primary goal of the interview, the reconstruction of a lived-through experience. The property of equifinality, therefore, serves as a caution to interviewers not to expect causal relationships in the communication process. Instead the expectation should be that the complex synchronic and diachronic features of the communicative event will emerge as various patterns depending upon the reciprocal episodic exchanges between the participants. Interviewers need to remain flexible and open to discoveries as the interview progresses.

In addition, the communication process is developmental in nature. As people communicate over time, the nature of their messages and of their relationship evolves. Any consideration of communication, therefore, must be done within the context of such potential evolution at the level of content and of relationship. This is because every message conveys information about two dimensions of the communication process: the content dimension and the relationship dimension.

In their classic work, *Pragmatics of Human Communication*, Watzlawick, Beavin, and Jackson pointed out the two-dimensional character of symbolic messages, saying that

any communication implies a commitment and thereby defines the relationship. This is another way of saying that a communication not only conveys information, but at the same time it imposes behavior. . . . The report aspect of a message conveys information and is, therefore, synonymous in human communication with the *content* of the message. . . . The command aspect, on the other hand, refers to what sort of message it is to be taken as, and, therefore, ultimately to the *relationship* between the communicants."[38]

From this view, then, interactional systems are taken to be "in the process of, or at the level of, defining the nature of their relationship."[39] The concern, of course, is with the dyadic relationship as mediated through communication. The mediation occurs, Watzlawick, Beavin and Jackson argue, through simultaneous use of "digital" and "analogic" cues: "Human beings communicate both digitally and analogically. Digital language has a highly complex and powerful logical syntax but lacks adequate semantics in the field of relationship, while analogic language possesses the semantics but has no adequate syntax for the unambiguous definition of the nature of relationships."[40]

Digital cues are equivalent to the linguistic code commonly referred to as language. This is the "content" dimension of messages. The analogic cues are constituted by the paralinguistic and extralinguistic features of the interactional system. These include nonverbal cues (e.g., body movement, silence, facial expressions), paralinguistic cues (e.g., voice tone and pitch), as well as context and refer to the "relationship" dimension of messages. Hence not only do interactants negotiate situated definitions about their intentions and meanings, but they also negotiate definitions of their relationship as constituted through the synchronic interaction. The human communication process is a developmental process, and that developmental process is best characterized as evolutionary.

The content and character of communication and the social realities it creates evolve and change over time. As people talk with one another from first meetings through mature relational stages to relationship termination, their communication changes in depth and in breadth and with these changes the nature of the relationship itself is modified. Thus, communication is a continually evolving process that changes us and our social world as we progress through time.[41]

For example, one of the first tasks in an interview is to build rapport. Typically, rapport is developed by asking easier questions first and holding more difficult ones for later. As was shown in the discussion of hermeneutical conversation, the interviews began with simple requests for information, built to requests for confirmation, then moved to mitigated challenges. All through the sequences, the interviewer nonverbally signaled support and cooperation.

HUMAN COMMUNICATION IS A CONTEXTUALLY GROUNDED PROCESS OF NEGOTIATING INTENTIONS, UNDERSTANDINGS, INTERPRETATIONS, AND MEANINGS. Throughout this book I have described the negotiation (such as rapport building) that occurs between interviewer and interviewee in elite oral history interviews; that is, the meanings emerge out of the interaction itself. For example, pause intervals within an utterance and between a question and an answer contribute to the emergence of meaning relative to the topic under discussion and relative to R and E's relationship.

I have also suggested that successful negotiation depends on collaboration between the interlocutors; that is, both parties must be knowledgeable of the conditions (e.g, rules and norms) under which negotiation can occur, and they must be willing to cooperate with each other toward achieving the goal of a successful interview.

Analysis of the interview discourse makes it clear that the negotiation process is contextually grounded. Furthermore, many of the most significant contextual variables are nonverbal, paralinguistic, and extralinguistic in nature. To probe the negotiation process, therefore, necessitates sensitivity to all of the contextual factors operating during a given interview. I have pointed out, for example, that supportive vocalic cues such as "((uh huh))" when interspersed appropriately in the respondent's answer contribute to setting a stage for cooperation even when difficult interchanges are occurring.

Explicit negotiation was discussed, for example, in the chapter on storytelling. In fact, storytelling was depicted as a process of negotiation and collaboration. The storyteller negotiates directly with the interviewer using management devices knowing that the interview is for the record, hence for a larger, more diverse audience.

Negotiation is also seen in the production of challenged and unchallenged records. In other words, what the record ultimately becomes depends on how R and E conduct their discussion of the lived-through event. That transaction is bound by verbal and nonverbal cues and by numerous other elements, such as the relationship between R and E, their respective goals, their interpretations, and their abilities.

Because each oral interview is a negotiated, developmental system, methods for evaluating the system must be developed. It no longer suffices to speak only of methods for evaluating the interview products. The collection process—oral, dyadic communication—must also be addressed. By so doing, oral historians are obliged to move beyond the traditional methods for evaluating documentary evidence; this move centers on the creative communication process, including both the content and the relationship levels of communication. Just as a complete view of human communication would necessarily include an account of the evolution of messages and relationships in time and through time, so depiction of the development of the content and relationship levels of communication as it occurs during the interview process should be considered essential to the oral history method. Although inclusion of audio and video recordings of the interview can suffice as part of that depiction, it may also be necessary for the interviewer and interviewee to include comments about their perceptions of the development of their relationship in time and through time. Examples of attempts at partial depiction of this developmental feature of the interview process are works by Oscar

Lewis, Harriet Zuckermen, and Peter Friedlander,[42] although not enough attention is given by these authors to the oral text and its creation. Depictions of the collection process should be included systematically in the body of materials considered as data. The tendency, however, is to discuss the product— usually the written record or by-products thereof—as opposed to the symbolic interaction that constitutes the collection process. A move in this direction by oral historians could serve as a foundation for developing evaluation methods for oral history interviewing.

The methodological issue involved with video recording in oral history seems to revolve around the tension between the need to preserve the full context of the interview and the need to create an unobtrusive interview setting. Each goal is an ideal that cannot be attained. However, degrees of each ideal can be reached. Unfortunately, there is an inverse relationship between the two goals. As steps are taken to capture fully the performance context, the more obtrusive the situation becomes. Likewise, efforts to reduce the intrusiveness of the situation result in the loss of access to the crucial nonverbal cues that are a part of the interview itself. Once this methodological decision is made, related issues of interpretation become salient. For the sake of illustration, I will examine some interpretational issues that must be considered whenever video recording is used to preserve the interview context.

The first issue can be identified by a caveat: the eye of the camera is not equivalent to the human eye. The eye of the camera cannot see the full peripheral range that is open to the human eye. In addition, the camera's view is of two-dimensional space. From the outset, then, video recording is beset with interpretational constraints. Awareness of the implications of the constraints can lead to informed decisions about the recording process. For example, the peripheral context of the interview could be captured through filming the setting before and after the interview. Interviewer and interviewee reactions to the setting could also be noted for future reference. This information could serve as interpretational aids for future viewers of the videotape.

Although the camera cannot be made to record in a three-dimensional spatial configuration, the seating arrangements of the interviewer and interviewee can be managed to capture the fullest view of the communication event. A crucial decision that impacts on interpretation is the number of cameras used to record the event. The oral historian must also decide the angle or line of the shot, the placement of the camera, and whether there will be a person operating the camera during the interview. Each decision impacts directly on the depiction of the interview in the video record. For example, the angle of the shot can impart a particular interpretation of a power relationship among the interviewer, the interviewee, and the viewer. Camera placement also impacts on this interpretation. If the camera is placed behind the shoulder of the interviewer, then the viewer sees the interaction through the interviewer's eyes, but the viewer misses the perspective of the interviewee. The opposite option of placing the camera over the shoulder of the interviewee would virtually eliminate the interviewee from the video record, a more unacceptable scenario. Over-the-shoulder camera placement does achieve a feeling of closeness relative to the interchange.

On the other hand, such intimacy is sacrificed if the camera is placed to film the face-to-face interchange. Here the interactants are seated virtually at right angles to the camera. In this way the nonverbal cues of both parties can be captured. A drawback to this arrangement is that the viewer and the camera might be more salient to the participants.

Finally, decisions about camera operation must be made. If there is no operator, then the entire recording will be static in terms of camera angle, distance, and placement. Movements by the interactants also would be more restricted. Such an arrangement can create a dull recording. By using a camera operator, the interviewer opens up the potential for creative filming techniques. Heightened creativity in the production of the videotape also heightens the producer's influence on subsequent interpretation of the record.

Even the simplest video recording techniques intrude into the interview. Such intrusion can be minimized depending upon the production decisions that are made. This is due primarily to the rapid advances in electronic communications technology. The trend is toward smaller, handheld equipment that can record using ordinary household illumination. Microphones are so sensitive that people no longer need to be connected to recording equipment. People, too, are becoming more sophisticated as users of video technology. In fact, anecdotal evidence suggests a willingness of people to be on camera.

Of course, all of these decisions that impact so markedly on interpretation of the video record are also constrained by logistical concerns such as accessibility of equipment, of appropriate filming locations, and of sufficient resources to pay for camera operators and videotapes. Time concerns as well as storage and maintenance of video records must also be considered. The decision to videotape oral history interviews is a complex one with numerous ramifications. At the heart of the decision is the perceived need to capture more fully the communicative interaction of the interview. To videotape or not to videotape will remain a thorny issue for oral historians.

One final communication-related issue needs to be addressed. That is the problem of editing. By editing I refer to all techniques used to translate the full audio/video recording of an oral history interview into some other form, for example, a book, a documentary video, a sound/slide production, a reader's theater presentation, or a dramatic play. Editing by definition implies transforming the original phenomenon into some altered form. The degree of alteration can vary from slight to extreme. Producers of oral history interview data must provide information (e.g., deposit raw data in archives) about the editing process used in creating the final product. By providing such information to users, the producers will be documenting their interpretational work in ways that audiences will find helpful.

I believe that guidelines for such documentation can be derived from the principles of communication set forth in this book. For purposes of illustration, I will address the fundamental editing issue that is derived from the nature of the oral history interview as an interactive, developmental process. The interview record emerges out of the interactive communicative process. The fundamental discourse unit of that process is the question/answer/third-turn response complex. Regardless of whether the interaction turns into stories or hermeneutical conversation, the outcome is still a joint product. The editing issue pertains to the tension between the goal of providing an authentic portrayal of the interactive, developmental process and the goal of creating an artistic product such as a video documentary. Although the trade-off between the goals is ultimately the decision of the producer/creator/ editor, I believe that the producer/creator/editor is obliged to reveal the original joint product. This is the only way informed critical judgments of products developed using oral history interview materials can be accomplished. Just as a writer documents the editing of a product via reference notes and bibliography, so a producer/creator/editor should document the editing of the interview interaction by making the original materials available to interested parties. In order to be true to the full context of the interview, the tapes as well as the transcripts of the interview must be available.

Summary

I have presented six principles of human communication theory that are essential for understanding oral history interviewing as an interpretive communicative event. These are:

Principle 1. A state of intersubjectivity is a precondition for human symbol-using activity.

Principle 2. Human communication is a creative process through which social (intersubjective) reality is constructed.

Principle 3. Human communication is a reason-based process.

Principle 4. Human communication takes place within a socio-historical context.

Principle 5. Human communication is an open system that is developmental in nature.

Principle 6. Human communication is a contextually grounded process of negotiating intentions, understandings, interpretations, and meanings.

Oral history interviewing is a creative process with the attendant promises and problems associated with the need to record the interview for the historical record. The interpretational issues associated with the oral interview method expand greatly as one shifts from audio recording to video recording. The two communication-related issues discussed here were the interpretational and editing problems associated with the oral interview method. These issues involve decisions about capturing the full performance context of the interview, the degree of intrusion necessary for capturing the communicative performances, and the relationship between the artistic freedom used in producing materials based on oral interviewing and the need for documenting the original interview interaction. All of these decisions need to be made within the context of the principles of human communication that underlie the oral interview method, because it is through communication that a personal, lived-through experience is transformed into a public, historical record.

Notes

Foreword

1. Jerome Bruner, "Life as Narrative," *Social Research* 54 (Spring 1987): 11–32.

2. Alice Kessler Harris, "Introduction," in *Envelopes of Sound: The Art of Oral History*, ed. Ronald J. Grele (Chicago: Precedent Publishing, 1985), 6–7.

3. Sidney W. Mintz, "The Anthropological Interview and the Life History," *Oral History Review* 7 (1979): 18–26; Francoise Morin, "Anthropological *Praxis* and Life History," trans. Kathleen Heffron, *International Journal of Oral History* 3 (February 1982): 5–30; Charles Joyner, "Oral History as Communicative Event: A Folkloristic Perspective," *Oral History Review* 7 (1979): 47–52; Paul Thompson, *The Voice of the Past: Oral History* (London: Oxford University Press, 1978); Charles D. Kaplan, "Addict Life Stories: An Exploration of the Methodological Grounds for the Study of Social Problems," *International Journal of Oral History* 3 (February 1982): 31–50 and (June 1982): 114–28.

4. E. Culpepper Clark, Michael J. Hyde, and Eva M. McMahan, "Communication in the Oral History Interview: Investigating Problems of Interpreting Oral Data," *International Journal of Oral History* 1 (February 1980): 28–40.

5. Ibid., 38.

Chapter 1

1. Luther C. Heinz, recorded interview by William W. Moss, 20 July 1970, pp. 4–5, John F. Kennedy Library Oral History Program, Boston.

2. The following discussion of philosophical hermeneutics and historical understanding is the product of several years of collaboration with E. Culpepper Clark of the University of Alabama and Michael J. Hyde of Northwestern University. I direct the reader to two essays that have directly influenced this discussion: E. Culpepper Clark, Michael J. Hyde, and Eva M. McMahan, "Communication in the Oral History Interview: Investigating Problems of Interpreting Oral Data," *International Journal of Oral History* 1 (February 1980): 28–40; and Michael J. Hyde, "Philosophical Hermeneutics and the Communicative Experience: The Paradigm of Oral History," *Man and World* 13 (1980): 81–98.

3. Hans-Georg Gadamer, *Truth and Method*, ed. Garrett Borden and John Cumming (New York: Continuum, 1975) and *Philosophical Hermeneutics*, ed. and trans. David E. Linge (Berkeley: University of California Press, 1976); Martin Heidegger, *Being and Time*, trans. John Macquarrie and Edward Robinson (New York: Harper and Row, 1962); Paul Ricoeur, *Interpretation Theory: Discourse and the Surplus of Meaning* (Fort Worth: Texas Christian University Press, 1976).

4. It is not my intention to engage in the debate about objective versus subjective meaning in historiography. The issue is introduced only to serve as a point of departure for philosophical hermeneutics as utilized in this book. For a discussion of historical objectivism, see E. D. Hirsch, Jr., *Validity in Interpretation* (New Haven: Yale University Press, 1967) and *The Aims of Interpretation* (Chicago: University of Chicago Press, 1976).

5. David Couzens Hoy, *The Critical Circle: Literature, History, and Philosophical Hermeneutics* (Berkeley: University of California Press, 1978), 14.

6. Joseph Kockelmans, "Toward an Interpretative or Hermeneutic Social Science," *New School for Social Research Graduate Faculty Philosophy Journal* 5 (Fall 1975): 83.

7. Clark, Hyde, and McMahan, "Communication in the Oral History Interview," 30.

8. Ibid.

9. Ibid.

10. Gadamer, *Truth and Method*, 276.

11. Kockelmans, "Toward an Interpretative or Hermeneutic Social Science," 75.

12. G. Ebeling, *The Problem of Historicity in the Church and its Proclamation* (Philadelphia: Fortress Press, 1967), 26.

13. Hoy, *The Critical Circle*, 41.

14. See Clark, Hyde, and McMahan, "Communication in the Oral History Interview," 31–32.

15. Ronald J. Grele, "Private Memories and Public Presentation: The Art

of Oral History," in *Envelopes of Sound: The Art of Oral History*, ed. Ronald J. Grele (Chicago: Precedent Publishing, 1985), 247.

16. Ibid., 246.

17. Hans Jonas, "Change and Permanence: On the Possibility of Understanding History," *Social Research* 38 (1971): 513.

18. Grele, "Private Memories and Public Presentation," 250.

19. Clark, Hyde, and McMahan, "Communication in the Oral History Interview," 31–32.

20. Kockelmans, "Toward an Interpretative or Hermeneutic Social Science," 86.

21. Barbara J. O'Keefe and Jesse G. Delia, "Psychological and Interactional Dimensions of Communicative Development," in *Recent Advances in Language, Communication, and Social Psychology*, ed. H. Giles and R. St. Clair (London: Lawrence Erlbaum, 1985), 48.

22. Hoy, *The Critical Circle*, 90.

23. O'Keefe and Delia, "Psychological and Interactional Dimensions," 48.

24. R. Rommetveit, *On Message Structure: A Framework for the Study of Language and Communication* (London: John Wiley and Sons, 1974), 63.

25. Some qualification of this point is necessary because neither party in the interview provides totally open feedback. We have to assume that each person maintains a public face during this process. Even so, the cues that are given off aid immeasurably in the overall interpretation of the interaction. The importance of the nonverbal cues for this issue is addressed more fully in chapter 5.

26. Gadamer, *Truth and Method*, 354.

27. Paul Thompson, "Life Histories and the Analysis of Social Change," in *Biography and Society: The Life History Approach in the Social Sciences*, ed. Daniel Bertaux (Beverly Hills, CA: Sage Publications, 1981), 294.

28. Gadamer, *Truth and Method*, 355.

29. David Henige, *Oral Historiography* (London: Longman, 1982), 122.

30. Robert P. Abelson, "Script Processing in Attitude Formation and Decision Making," in *Cognition and Social Behavior*, ed. John S. Carroll and John W. Payne (Potomac, MD: Lawrence Erlbaum, 1976), 33–45.

31. Clark, Hyde, and McMahan, "Communication in the Oral History Interview," 32.

32. Ibid.

33. Kockelmans, "Toward an Interpretative or Hermeneutic Social Science," 92.

34. Daniel Bertaux, "Stories as Clues to Sociological Understanding: The Bakers of Paris," in *Our Common History: The Transformation of Europe*, ed. Paul Thompson (London: Pluto Press, 1982), 98.

35. O'Keefe and Delia, "Psychological and Interactional Dimensions," 53.

36. Schutz distinguishes between "ideally rational action" and "rational action on the common-sense level." Ideally rational action "presupposes that the actor has clear and distinct insight into the ends, the means, and the secondary results, which involves rational consideration of alternative means to the end, to the relations of the end to other prospective results of employment of any given means, and, finally, of the relative importance of

different possible ends" (p. 28). Schutz contends that while ideally rational action might be possible for one individual to attain, it is virtually impossible to project ideally rational action in human relationships because even consociates do not possess sufficient knowledge of each other's "projects" to achieve such understanding. Thus Schutz proposes commonsense rational action as an alternative construct for explaining goal-directed human behavior. Alfred Schutz, "Common-Sense and Scientific Interpretation of Human Action," *Collected Papers I: The Problem of Social Reality*, ed. Maurice Natanson (The Hague: Martinus Nijhoff, 1967), 27–34.

37. Ibid., 33.

38. For example, see Roman Harre, "Some Remarks on 'Rule' as a Scientific Concept," in *Understanding Other Persons*, ed. Theodore Mischel (Totowa, NJ: Rowman and Littlefield, 1974), 143–84; Harre and Paul Secord, *The Explanation of Social Behavior* (Oxford: Basil Blackwell, 1972); Stephen Toulmin, "Rules and Their Relevance for Understanding Human Behavior," in *Understanding Other Persons*, ed. Mischel, 185–215.

39. Harre, "Some Remarks on 'Rule,' " 152.

40. Schutz, "Common-Sense and Scientific Interpretation," 32. This does not mean that all action will be rule-following behavior. It means that actions are considered in terms of the rules. Likewise, there may not be full awareness of all of the applicable rules in a given situation.

41. Harre, "Some Remarks on 'Rule,' " 151.

42. J. L. Austin, *How to Do Things with Words* (Cambridge, MA: Harvard University Press, 1962); John R. Searle, *Speech Acts: An Essay in the Philosophy of Language* (Cambridge: Cambridge University Press, 1969).

43. For a different conception of the structure of the oral history interview, see Ronald J. Grele, "Movement without Aim: Methodological and Theoretical Problems in Oral History," in *Envelopes of Sound*, ed. Ronald J. Grele, 126–54 (Chicago: Precedent Publishing, 1985); and "Private Memories and Public Presentation," 242–83.

44. H. P. Grice, "Logic and Conversation," in *Syntax and Semantics*, Vol. 3: *Speech Acts*, ed. P. Cole and J. L. Morgan (New York: Academic Press, 1975), 45–47.

45. This view, of course, is derived from the pioneering work of J. L. Austin, who claimed that the issuing of an utterance is equivalent to the performing of an action. Such utterances are labeled *performatives*. This idea has formed the centerpiece for speech act theory. See, for example, Austin, *How to Do Things with Words*, and Searle, *Speech Acts*.

46. Eva M. McMahan, "Communicative Dynamics of Hermeneutical Conversation in Oral History Interviews," *Communication Quarterly* 31 (Winter 1983): 3–11.

47. Grele, "Movement without Aim," 126–54.

48. Hyde, "Philosophical Hermeneutics and the Communicative Experience," 91–93.

49. Alfred Schutz, *The Phenomenology of the Social World*, edited by John Wild, translated by George Walsh and Frederick Lehnert (Evanston, IL: Northwestern University Press, 1967), 74.

50. Ibid.

51. McMahan, "Communicative Dynamics," 4.

52. It is this concept of conflict that Barbara Allen has misconstrued. Her analysis is flawed in this way: (1) The diachronic nature of historical understanding is much more complex and densely layered with meaning than her analysis suggests. The difference between interviewer and interviewee is much deeper than merely the difference between "first-hand" and "second-hand" experience. Thus her redefinition of the term *conflict* is not a sufficient alternative definition given the hermeneutical nature of oral history. (2) There is a misinterpretation of the potential for oral history interviewing to become dialectical. As the model presented in this chapter suggests, resolution of different meanings of the historical event in question is only one of several possible outcomes. Moreover, Allen implies that we have defined a successful interview as one that resolves conflicts through dialectic. Such a suggestion is inconsistent with the theoretical approach taken here. In fact, a more appropriate metaphor would be Gadamer's "fusion of horizons." See Barbara Allen, "Recreating the Past: The Narrator's Perspective in Oral History," *Oral History Review* 12 (1984): 1–12.

53. McMahan, "Communicative Dynamics," 5.

54. Gadamer, *Truth and Method*, 330–31.

55. Kockelmans, "Toward An Interpretative or Hermeneutic Social Science," 93.

56. McMahan, "Communicative Dynamics," 5–11.

57. Ibid., 6.

Chapter 2

1. Stafford Warren, recorded interview by Ronald J. Grele, 7 June 1966, pp. 26–27, John F. Kennedy Library Oral History Program, Boston.

2. For a discussion of the interviewer's role in news interviews, see John Heritage, "Analyzing News Interviews: Aspects of the Production of Talk for an Overhearing Audience," in *Handbook of Discourse Analysis*, ed. Teun Van Dijk (London: Academic Press, 1985), 95–119.

3. Schutz, *Phenomenology of the Social World*, and "Common-Sense and Scientific Interpretation"; Aaron Cicourel, *Cognitive Sociology: Language and Meaning in Social Interaction* (London: Cox and Wyman, 1973); Austin, *How to Do Things with Words*; Searle, *Speech Acts*; Paul Ricoeur, *Interpretation Theory*, and "The Model of the Text: Meaningful Action Considered as a Text," *New Literary History* 5 (1973): 91–117; Harre and Secord, *Explanation of Social Behavior*; B. A. Mohan, "Do Sequencing Rules Exist?" *Semiotica* 12 (1974): 75–96; Scott Jacobs and Sally Jackson, "Speech Act Structure in Conversation: Rational Aspects of Pragmatic Coherence," in *Conversational Coherence: Form, Structure, and Strategy*, ed. Robert T. Craig and Karen Tracy (Beverly Hills, CA: Sage Publications, 1983), 47–66; William Labov and David Fanshel, *Therapeutic Discourse* (New York: Academic Press, 1977); Kent Bach and Robert M. Harnish, *Linguistic Com-*

munication and Speech Acts (Cambridge, MA: MIT Press, 1979); R. Harre, "Some Remarks on 'Rule.' "

4. For a discussion of this "question-and-answer complex," see R. G. Collingwood, *An Autobiography* (London: Oxford University Press, 1939).

5. Michael Stubbs, *Discourse Analysis: The Sociolinguistic Analysis of Natural Language* (Chicago: University of Chicago Press, 1983), 15.

6. John J. Gumperz and D. Hymes, eds., *Directions in Sociolinguistics* (New York: Holt, Rinehart, and Winston, 1972); Erving Goffman, *Strategic Interaction* (Philadelphia: University of Pennsylvania Press, 1969); Harvey Sacks, "On the Analyzability of Stories by Children," in *Directions in Sociolinguistics*, ed. Gumperz and Hymes, 325–45; Emmanuel Schegloff, "Sequencing in Conversational Openings," in *Directions in Sociolinguistics*, ed. Gumperz and Hymes, 346–80; Austin, *How to Do Things with Words*; Searle, *Speech Acts*; H. P. Grice, "Logic and Conversation," 45; Labov and Fanshel, *Therapeutic Discourse*; Jacobs and Jackson, "Speech Act Structure"; Robert E. Nofsinger, Jr., "On Answering Questions Indirectly: Some Rules in the Grammar of Doing Conversation," *Human Communication Research* 2 (1976): 172–81; Bach and Harnish, *Linguistic Communication and Speech Acts*.

7. Stubbs, *Discourse Analysis*, 15.

8. Ibid., 30.

9. Discourse analysis is not limited to the study of naturally occurring discourse.

10. Excellent overviews of the various approaches to discourse analysis can be found in Margaret L. McLaughlin, *Conversation: How Talk Is Organized* (Beverly Hills, CA: Sage Publications, 1984); Craig and Tracy, eds., *Conversational Coherence*; and J. Schenkein, ed., *Studies in the Organization of Conversational Interaction* (New York: Academic Press, 1978).

11. Rules-based explanations vary somewhat according to author. See, for example, Susan Shimanoff, *Communication Rules: Theory and Research* (Beverly Hills, CA: Sage Publications, 1980); Harre and Secord, *Explanation of Social Behavior*; Joan S. Ganz, *Rules: A Systematic Study* (The Hague: Mouton, 1971); Mary John Smith, *Persuasion and Human Action: A Review and Critique of Social Influence Theories* (Belmont, CA: Wadsworth, 1982); P. Collett, "The Rules of Conduct," in *Social Rules and Social Behavior*, ed. P. Collett (Totowa, NJ: Rowman and Littlefield, 1977), 1–27; Stephen Toulmin, "Rules and Their Relevance for Understanding Human Behavior"; Harre, "Some Remarks on 'Rule' "; and Bach and Harnish, *Linguistic Communication and Speech Acts*.

12. McLaughlin, *Conversation*, 17.

13. Grice, "Logic and Conversation," 45.

14. McLaughlin, *Conversation*, 32.

15. See, for example, Austin, *How to Do Things with Words*; and Searle, *Speech Acts*.

16. Norman Denzin, "Introduction to Problems of Design and Analysis," in *Sociological Methods: A Sourcebook*, ed. Norman K. Denzin (Chicago: Aldine, 1970), 218.

17. McLaughlin, *Conversation*, 48.

18. Grice, "Logic and Conversation," 45–47.

19. Thompson, *Voice of the Past*, 182.

20. Eva M. McMahan, "Speech and Counterspeech: Language-In-Use in Oral History Fieldwork," *Oral History Review* 15 (Spring 1987): 185–208. Also see John Heritage, "Analyzing News Interviews."

21. Heritage, "Analyzing News Interviews." It is important to note that all three devices serve pragmatically as speech acts, that is, requests.

22. Ibid., 105.

23. Stafford Warren, recorded interview by Ronald J. Grele, 7 June 1966, pp. 26–27, John F. Kennedy Library Oral History Program, Boston.

24. Peter H. B. Frelinghuysen, recorded interview by Ronald J. Grele, 7 June 1966, pp. 29–34, New Jersey Historical Commission Oral History Program.

25. Heritage, "Analyzing News Interviews," 108.

26. Peter H. B. Frelinghuysen, recorded interview by Ronald J. Grele, 29 September 1978, pp. 101–2, New Jersey Historical Commission Oral History Program.

27. Ibid., 76–79.

28. Bach and Harnish, *Linguistic Communication and Speech Acts*, 64; P. Brown and S. Levinson, "Universals in Language Usage: Politeness Phenomena," in *Questions and Politeness: Strategies in Social Interaction*, ed. E. Goody (Cambridge: Cambridge University Press, 1978), 56–289.

29. Jacobs and Jackson, "Speech Act Structure," 34–55.

30. McLaughlin, *Conversation*, 137.

31. According to Austin, the conditions for the happy functioning of a performative are: (1) There must exist an accepted conventional procedure having a certain conventional effect, that procedure to include the uttering of certain words by certain persons in certain circumstances, and further, the particular persons and circumstances in a given case must be appropriate for the invocation of the particular procedure invoked. (2) The procedure must be executed by all participants both correctly and completely. (3) Where, as often, the procedure is designed for use by persons having certain thoughts or feelings, or for the inauguration of certain consequential conduct on the part of any participant, then a person participating in and so invoking the procedure must in fact have those thoughts or feelings, and the participants must intend so to conduct themselves, and further must actually so conduct themselves subsequently. *How to Do Things with Words*, 14–15.

32. For example, see Labov and Fanshel, *Therapeutic Discourse*, and McLaughlin, *Conversation*.

33. Bach and Harnish, *Linguistic Communication*; Brown and Levinson, "Universals in Language Usage," 56–289.

34. McLaughlin, *Conversation*, 137.

35. Ibid., 160.

36. McLaughlin, *Conversation*; Craig and Tracy, *Conversational Coherence*; and Schenkein, *Studies in the Organization of Conversational Interaction*.

37. The rule of requests is: "If A (speaker) requests (B) to perform an

action X at a time, T, A's utterance will be heard as a valid command only if the following pre-conditions hold: B believes that A believes (1) X should be done for a purpose Y; (2) B has the ability to do X; (3) B has the obligation to do X; (4) A has the right to tell B to do X." Labov and Fanshel, *Therapeutic Discourse*, 70.

38. In the context of the oral history interview, the rule of requests is pertinent to the case where an interviewer (R) requests an interviewee (E) to perform an action (X) relevant to the interviewer's purpose. The role of interviewer legitimizes R's right to request an action. The interviewee's role means that E has an obligation to do X.

39. Transformed to the oral history interview setting, the rule of request for information would read: If an interviewer (R) addresses to an interviewee (E) an imperative requesting information about a historical event (Z) or an interrogative focusing on Z, then R's utterance will be heard as a valid request for information if the following preconditions hold: E believes that R believes that: (1) information about Z should be given for the purpose Y (where Y is to re-create E's lived-through experience); (2) E has the ability to give information about Z; (3) E has the obligation to give information about Z; and (4) R has the right to ask E to give information about Z. This is a modification of the preconditions for the rule of request as found in Labov and Fanshel, *Therapeutic Discourse*, 89. Here, R may already have the information requested but may want E's answer on the record.

40. The rule of indirect request reads: "If A makes to B a request for information or an assertion to B about (a) the existential status of an action S to be performed by B; (b) the consequences of performing an action X; (c) the time T that an action S might be performed by B; (d) any of the pre-conditions for a valid request for X as given in the rule of requests and all other pre-conditions are in effect, then A is heard as making a valid request of B for the action X." Labov and Fanshel, *Therapeutic Discourse*, 82. In the oral history interview situation, the rule of indirect request for information can be read: If R makes to E a request for information or an assertion about (a) the status of knowledge of E about Z; (b) the status of knowledge of R about Z; (c) any of the preconditions for a valid request for information as given in the rule of request for information and all other preconditions are in effect, then R is heard as making a valid request for information about Z.

41. Peter Lisagor, recorded interview by Ronald J. Grele, 22 April 1966, pp. 7–8, John F. Kennedy Library Oral History Program, Boston.

42. Lisagor interview, 36.

43. The rule of indirect request for permission to provide information is: Whenever E makes an assertion to R, or addresses an interrogative to R, about (a) the status of knowledge of E about Z or (b) the status of knowledge of R about Z *and* E believes that R believes that (c) information about Z should be provided for a valid purpose, (d) E has the ability to provide information about Z, (e) E has the right to request for permission to suggest that Z be discussed, (f) R has the right to grant or refuse the request, then such an indirect request for permission to provide information about Z is heard as a valid request for permission to provide information about Z.

44. Lisagor interview, 10.

45. The rule of request for confirmation is: If R makes a statement about Z, then it is heard as a request for confirmation of the statement. This is a significant departure from the rule of confirmation proposed by Labov and Fanshel. This is because their classification of statements according to the shared knowledge involved—A-events, A-B-events, O-events, and D-events—is based on the assumption that some events are a priori indisputable. My position—derived from philosophical hermeneutics—is that all events are potentially disputable. Hence no classification of $Z_1 \ldots Z_n$ in such terms is necessary. For the viewpoint of Labov and Fanshel, see *Therapeutic Discourse*, 100–101.

46. William Howell, recorded interview by Ronald J. Grele, 4 February 1970, pp. 29–31, New Jersey Historical Commission Oral History Program.

47. Labov and Fanshel, *Therapeutic Discourse*, 91. The rule of embedded request when applied to the oral history interview is: If R makes a request for information to E about Z, and E responds with a request for information, E is heard as asserting that he or she needs that information in order to respond to R's request.

48. Howard Palfrey Jones, recorded interview by Dennis O'Brien, 23 June 1969, p. 2, John F. Kennedy Library Oral History Program, Boston.

49. The rule of putting off requests is: "If A has made a valid request for the action X of B and B addresses to A: (a) a positive assertion or request for information about the existential status of X; (b) a request for information or negative assertion about the Time; (c) a request for information or negative assertion about one of the four pre-conditions, then B is heard as refusing the request until the information is supplied or the negative assertion is contradicted." Labov and Fanshel, *Therapeutic Discourse*, 86–87.

50. Joe W. Burleson, recorded interview by E. Culpepper Clark, 2 August 1978, p. 48, University of Alabama, Department of Speech Communication.

51. Howell interview, 46–47.

Chapter 3

1. Luther C. Heinz, recorded interview by William W. Moss, 27 July 1970, pp. 48–50, John F. Kennedy Library Oral History Program, Boston.

2. McMahan, "Communicative Dynamics," 5.

3. Hyde, "Philosophical Hermeneutics and the Communicative Experience," 92.

4. Sally Jackson and Scott Jacobs, "Structure of Conversational Argument: Pragmatic Bases for the Enthymeme," *Quarterly Journal of Speech* 66 (1980): 254.

5. Ibid., 251.

6. Ibid., 252.

7. Ibid., 252.

8. Ibid., 254.

9. Heinz interview, 20 July 1970, pp. 2–3.

10. McMahan, "Communicative Dynamics," 10.

11. Ibid.

12. Heinz interview, 27 July 1970, pp. 48–50.

13. Douglas V. Johnson, recorded interview by William W. Moss, 13 July 1970, pp. 9–10, John F. Kennedy Library Oral History Program, Boston.

14. Gadamer, *Truth and Method*, 331.

15. Ibid.

16. I am grateful to Scott Jacobs for insights about this issue.

17. McMahan, "Communicative Dynamics," 9.

18. The rule of admitting disputability of events: "If A makes an assertion which calls into question an interpretation of an event (Z), and if B responds to the assertion without mentioning the presuppositions or implications underlying the assertion, then B admits those presuppositions or implications, hence the disputability of the interpretation." McMahan, "Communicative Dynamics," 10.

19. The rule of disputable assertions: "If A makes an assertion about a D-event, it is heard as a request for B to give an evaluation of that assertion." Labov and Fanshel, *Therapeutic Discourse*, 101.

20. Heinz interview, 20 July 1970, pp. 5–7.

21. Heinz interview, 20 July 1970, pp. 10–11.

22. Joseph B. Drachnik, recorded interview by William W. Moss, 27 July 1970, pp. 4–6, John F. Kennedy Library Oral History Program, Boston.

23. Johnson interview, pp. 12–14.

24. Heinz interview, 20 July 1970, pp. 13–15.

Chapter 4

1. Livia Polanyi, "Conversational Storytelling," in *Handbook of Discourse Analysis*, Vol. 3, ed. Teun Van Dijk (London: Academic Press, 1985), 189.

2. See, for example, Harvey Sacks, "On The Analysability of Stories by Children," in *Directions in Sociolinguistics*, ed. Gumperz and Hymes, 325–45 (New York: Holt, Rinehart and Winston, 1972).

3. Polanyi, "Conversational Storytelling," 200.

4. Ibid., 187.

5. Gail Jefferson, "Sequential Aspects of Storytelling in Conversation," in *Studies in the Organization of Conversational Interaction*, ed. Jim Schenkein (New York: Academic Press, 1978), 220.

6. Polanyi, "Conversational Storytelling," 200.

7. Lisagor interview, 22 April 1966, pp. 14–19.

8. Labov and Fanshel, *Therapeutic Discourse*, 109.

9. Ibid., 104–11.

10. Ibid., 106.

11. Ibid.

12. Ibid., 107.

Chapter 5

1. Schutz, "Common-Sense and Scientific Interpretation," 10.
2. Rommetveit, *On Message Structure*, 23.
3. Schutz, "Common-Sense and Scientific Interpretation," 12.
4. Ibid.
5. Ibid., 14.
6. Rommetveit, *On Message Structure*, 37.
7. Searle, *Speech Acts*, 50.
8. Jesse G. Delia and Larry Grossberg, "Interpretation and Evidence," *Western Journal of Speech Communication* (Winter 1977): 36.
9. Herbert Blumer, "Society as Symbolic Interaction," in *Symbolic Interaction: A Reader in Social Psychology*, ed. Jerome G. Manis and Bernard N. Meltzer (Boston: Allyn and Bacon, 1978), 97–103.
10. Schutz, "On Multiple Realities," *Collected Papers I*, 210.
11. O'Keefe and Delia, "Psychological and Interactional Dimensions," 64–65.
12. Ibid., 64.
13. Ibid., 65.
14. Rommetveit, *On Message Structure*, 52.
15. Schutz, "Common-Sense and Scientific Interpretation," 23.
16. Mary John Smith, *Contemporary Communication Research Methods* (Belmont, CA: Wadsworth, 1988), 305.
17. Thompson, *The Voice of the Past*, x.
18. Smith, *Contemporary Communication Research Methods*, 312.
19. Ibid., 313.
20. Shimanoff, *Communication Rules*, 32.
21. Smith, *Contemporary Communication Research Methods*, 312–13.
22. Kenneth Burke, *The Rhetoric of Religion* (Boston: Beacon Press, 1961), 40–41.
23. Harre and Secord, *Explanation of Social Behavior*, 35.
24. Perhaps Shimanoff's characterization of the structure of these means-end relationships in terms of the Toulmin model is even more instructive. The goal-action linkage is portrayed structurally wherein the context is the data, the linkage or rule is the warrant for connecting the context to the action, and the warrant or rule is backed by evidence of the existence of the linkage. The reservation for the warrant, the "unless," indicates the possibility that the goal-action linkage may be invalidated by certain mitigating factors. Shimanoff, *Communication Rules*, 232–34.
25. "To explain communicative behaviors occurring at lower levels of awareness, rules theorists rely on a form of teleological explanation called the teleonomic script rule or programmatic perspective. From the programmatic view, people's reasons for communicating are embedded in scripts, defined as 'prearranged information that controls a process (or behavior) leading it toward a given end. . . . ' A teleonomic script contains programmed goals, instructions for achieving the goals, and prescriptions for dealing with internal and external disruption of the process leading to the goals. Thus,

program or teleonomic scripts allow us to communicate purposively, yet avoid continuous deliberation about our reasons for communicating. Whereas both the intentional and programmatic views address the motivations of individual communicators, the systems rule focuses on the interrelatedness of communicators belonging to 'the social system as a whole. . . . ' From the systems perspective, people's communicative behaviors are explained by referring to systemic goals, that is, the collective objectives shared by a group of communicators. A systems analysis explores how individual messages contribute to systemic goals and how a system's rule structure affects individual communication patterns." Smith, *Contemporary Communication Research Methods*, 314.

26. George Herbert Mead, *Mind, Self, and Society*, ed. Charles W. Morris (Chicago: University of Chicago Press, 1934).

27. O'Keefe and Delia, "Psychological and Interactional Dimensions," 48–49.

28. Delia and Grossberg, "Interpretation and Evidence," 36.

29. R. L. Birdwhistell, cited in Rommetveit, *On Message Structure*, 62.

30. Ronald J. Grele, "A Surmisable Variety: Interdisciplinarity and Oral Testimony," in *Envelopes of Sound*, ed. Ronald J. Grele (Chicago: Precedent Publishing, 1985), 162–63.

31. Grele, "A Surmisable Variety," 183.

32. Ibid., 163.

33. Joyner, "Oral History as Communicative Event," 48.

34. Grele, "A Surmisable Variety," 165.

35. For example, see John W. Sutherland, *A General Systems Philosophy for the Social and Behavioral Sciences* (New York: George Braziller, 1973).

36. Paul Watzlawick, Janet Beavin, and Don D. Jackson, *Pragmatics of Human Communication* (New York: W. W. Norton, 1967), 125.

37. Smith, *Contemporary Communication Research Methods*, 306.

38. Watzlawick, Beavin, and Jackson, *Pragmatics of Human Communication*, 51–52.

39. Ibid., 121.

40. Ibid., 66–67.

41. Smith, *Contemporary Communication Research Methods*, 305–6.

42. Oscar Lewis, *The Children of Sanchez: Autobiography of a Mexican Family* (New York: Random House, 1961); Harriet Zuckerman, *Scientific Elite: Nobel Laureates in the United States* (New York: Free Press, 1977); Peter Friedlander, *The Emergence of a UAW Local, 1936–1939: A Study in Class and Culture* (Pittsburgh: University of Pittsburgh Press, 1975).

Glossary

———————————————————————

Adjacency pair: a two-part conversational turn structure wherein the first pair-part (FPP) establishes a next turn position that is expected to be filled by an appropriate second pair-part (SPP)

Analogic cues: the nonverbal code

Articulated conflict at the functional level: withholding of a preferred second pair-part and the failure to withdraw or suppress the disagreeable first pair-part in the adjacency pair structure of conversational turns

Articulated conflict at the propositional level: the display of differing points of view in the adjacency pair structure of conversational turns

Bracketing: an organizational management device that functions to mark out units of discourse

Coherence: local, global, and themal relatedness of discourse

Conflict: the inherent perspectives, or different conceptions of the past, that the interlocutors bring to the discussion of the historical event

Contradiction: each interactant affirms her or his own perception of the historical event, which in turn results in disagreement

Contrariety: both the interviewer and interviewee maintain their separate understandings, interpretations, and meanings of any feature of the historical event while acknowledging the potential validity of the other's perception

Cooperative principle: show cooperation with your conversational partner

Cooperative recycle: an interviewer's restatement of the interviewee's prior talk

Digital cues: the linguistic code

Disputable assertion: a statement that provides an alternative interpretation of the subject

Elite: persons who develop a lore that justifies their attempts to control society

Equifinality: the same goal can be reached in different ways from different starting points

Formulation: a device used by a speaker to place sequences of talk or episodes into a larger organizational framework

Hermeneutical conversation: the art of conversation that enables both conversational partners to work out a new meaning

Illocution: what is done in the act of saying something

Imagined audience: the potential users of the oral history data

Inferentially elaborative probe: thematizing some presupposition of prior talk that the interviewer proposes is implied in that talk or its real world context

Interpretive rule: a statement that sets forth the conditions that must be present in order for an utterance to count as a particular kind of proposition or a particular type of illocution

Locution: what is said

Mitigated challenges: a class of illocutions wherein the interviewer calls into question the interviewee's answer without assessing the interviewee's competence as an informed reporter of her or his lived-through experience

Nonsummativity: the whole is greater than the sum of its parts

Nonverbal communication: messages without words, including vocalic cues, voice tone and rhythm, and body language

Oral history: an interview/conversation with a person whose life experience is regarded as memorable

Paralanguage: the cues in oral discourse excluding the content of the spoken words

Performative: language as action

Perlocution: the effect produced by the illocution

Prompt: a minor inference by the interviewer based on prior statements by the interviewee

Proposition: the content of the utterance

Requests: a class of illocutions that solicits action from the listener

Rule: a statement that models the ways in which social interaction should be constituted and executed

Story: a narrative about the past that makes a point

Third-turn response: the interviewer's response to the second pair-part of a question-answer adjacency pair

Turn-taking: the process of alternating roles as speaker and listener in an interview/conversation

Bibliography

Aaron, Daniel. *Writers on the Left, Episodes in American Literature.* New York: Harcourt, Brace, and World, 1961.

Abelson, Robert P. "Script Processing in Attitude Formation and Decision Making." In *Cognition and Social Behavior*, edited by John S. Carroll and John W. Payne, 33–45. Potomac, MD: Lawrence Erlbaum, 1976.

Agar, Michael H. *Speaking of Ethnography.* Beverly Hills, CA: Sage Publications, 1986.

Allen, Barbara. *From Memory to History: Using Oral Sources in Local History Research.* Nashville: American Association for State and Local History, 1981.

———. "Recreating the Past: The Narrator's Perspective in Oral History." *Oral History Review* 12 (1984): 1–12.

———. "In the Thick of Things: Texture in Orally Communicated History." *International Journal of Oral History* 6 (1985): 92–103.

Allen, Richard B. "New Orleans Jazz Archive at Tulane." *Wilson Library Bulletin* 40 (1965–66): 619–23.

Allen, Susan Emily. "Resisting the Editorial Ego: Editing Oral History." *Oral History Review* 10 (1982): 33–45.

Ancelet, Barry Jean. "And This Is No Damn Lie: Oral History in Story Form." *International Journal of Oral History* 4 (June 1983): 99–111.

Arkin, Stephen. "Composing the Self: The Literary Interview as

Form." *International Journal of Oral History* 4 (February 1983): 12–18.

Armitage, Susan H. "The Next Step." *Frontiers* 7 (1983): 3–8.

Atkinson, J. Maxwell, and John Heritage, eds. *Structures of Social Action: Studies in Conversation Analysis.* Cambridge: Cambridge University Press, 1984.

Austin, J. L. *How to Do Things with Words.* Cambridge, MA: Harvard University Press, 1962.

Bach, Kent, and Robert M. Harnish. *Linguistic Communication and Speech Acts.* Cambridge, MA: MIT Press, 1979.

Bakker, Nelleke, and Jrap Talsma. "Women and Work Between the Wars: The Amsterdam Seamstresses." In *Our Common History: The Transformation of Europe,* edited by Paul Thompson, 171–84. London: Pluto Press, 1982.

Ballmer, T., and W. Brennenstuhl. *Speech Act Classification: A Study in the Lexical Analysis of English Speech Activity Verbs.* New York: Springer-Verlag, 1981.

Balthrop, V. William. "Argumentation and the Critical Stance." In *Advances in Argumentation Theory and Research,* edited by J. Robert Cox and Charles Arthur Willard, 238–58. Carbondale, IL: Southern Illinois University Press, 1982.

Banaka, William H. *Training In Depth Interviewing.* New York: Harper and Row, 1970.

Barnet, Miguel. *Gallego.* Madrid, 1981.

Barzun, Jacques, and Henry Graff. *The Modern Researcher.* Rev. ed. New York: Harcourt, Brace, Jovanovich, 1970.

Baum, Willa K. *Oral History for the Local Historical Society.* Nashville: American Association for State and Local History, 1974.

―――. *Transcribing and Editing Oral History.* Nashville: American Association for State and Local History, 1977.

Beier, Ulli. *Yoruba Myths.* London: Cambridge University Press, 1980.

Bell, Jack. Recorded Interview by Joseph E. O'Conner. 19 April 1966, pp. 22–23. John F. Kennedy Library Oral History Program, Boston.

Benjamin, Alfred. *The Helping Interview.* Boston: Houghton Mifflin, 1969.

Benjamin, Walter. *Illuminations.* New York: Harcourt, Brace and World, 1968.

―――. "On Interviewing: Excerpts from 'The Storyteller.' " *International Journal of Oral History* 2 (1981): 195–204.

Benmayor, Rina. Review of *Our Common History: The Transformation of Europe,* edited by Paul Thompson. *International Journal of Oral History* 4 (1983): 190–200.

Bennett, James. *Oral History and Delinquency: The Rhetoric of Criminology.* Chicago: University of Chicago Press, 1981.

———. "Human Values in Oral History." *Oral History Review* 11 (1983): 1–16.

Bertaux, Daniel, ed. *Biography and Society: The Life History Approach in the Social Sciences.* Beverly Hills, CA: Sage Publications, 1981.

———. "From the Life History Approach to the Transformation of Sociological Practice." In *Biography and Society,* edited by Daniel Bertaux, 29–45. Beverly Hills, CA: Sage Publications, 1981.

———. "Stories as Clues to Sociological Understanding: The Bakers of Paris." In *Our Common History: The Transformation of Europe,* edited by Paul Thompson, 93–108. London: Pluto Press, 1982.

Bertaux, Daniel, and Isabelle Bertaux-Waime. "Life Stories in the Baker's Trade." In *Biography and Society,* edited by Daniel Bertaux, 169–89. Beverly Hills, CA: Sage Publications, 1981.

Bertaux-Waime, Isabelle. "The Life History Approach to the Study of Internal Migration." In *Biography and Society,* edited by Daniel Bertaux, 249–65. Beverly Hills, CA: Sage Publications, 1981.

———. "The Life History Approach to the Study of Internal Migration: How Women and Men Came to Paris Between the Wars." In *Our Common History: The Transformation of Europe,* edited by Paul Thompson, 186–200. London: Pluto Press, 1982.

Bierstedt, Robert, ed. *Florian Znaniecki on Humanistic Sociology.* Chicago: University of Chicago Press, 1969.

Bingham, Walter Van Dyke, and Bruce Victor Moore. *How to Interview.* New York: Harper and Brothers, 1959.

Blumer, Herbert. "Society as Symbolic Interaction." In *Symbolic Interaction: A Reader in Social Psychology,* edited by Jerome G. Manis and Bernard N. Meltzer, 97–103. Boston: Allyn and Bacon, 1978.

Blythin, Evan, and Larry A. Samovar. *Communicating Effectively on Television.* Belmont, CA: Wadsworth, 1985.

Bogdan, Robert, and Steve J. Taylor. *Introduction to Qualitative Research Methods.* New York: John Wiley and Sons, 1975.

Borderias, Cristina, and Mercedes Vilanova. "Memories of Hope and Defeat: Catalan Miners and Fishermen Under the Second Spanish Republic, 1931–9." In *Our Common History: The Transformation of Europe,* edited by Paul Thompson, 38–53. London: Pluto Press, 1982.

Botkin, Benjamin A., ed. *Lay My Burden Down: A Folk History of Slavery.* Chicago: University of Chicago Press, 1945.

———. "Applied Folklore: Creating Understanding Through Folklore." *Southern Folklore Quarterly* 17, no. 3 (September 1953): 199–207.

Bowers, J. W. "Does a Duck Have Antlers? Some Pragmatics of 'Transparent Questions.'" *Communication Monographs* 49 (1982): 63–69.

Bracey, John H., Jr., et al. *Black Workers and Organized Labor*. Belmont, CA: Wadsworth, 1971.

Bradley, P. H. "The Folk-linguistics of Women's Speech: An Empirical Examination." *Communication Monographs* 48 (1981): 73–90.

Bradshaw, John. "Oral Transmission and Human Memory." *The Expository Times* 92 (July 1981): 303–7.

Bravo, Anna. "Solidarity and Loneliness: Piedmontese Peasant Women at the Turn of the Century." *International Journal of Oral History* 3 (1982): 76–91.

———. "Italian Peasant Women and the First World War." In *Our Common History: The Transformation of Europe*, edited by Paul Thompson, 157–70. London: Pluto Press, 1982.

Brenner, Michael, Jennifer Brown, and David Canter, eds. *The Research Interview: Uses and Approaches*. London: Academic Press, 1985.

Briggs, Charles L. *Learning How to Ask: A Sociolinguistic Appraisal of the Role of the Interview in Social Science Research*. Cambridge: Cambridge University Press, 1986.

Brockriede, Wayne. "Characteristics of Arguments and Arguing." *Journal of the American Forensic Association* 13 (1977): 129–32.

Broughton, Irv. *The Art of Interviewing for Television, Radio, and Film*. Blue Ridge Summit, PA: Tab Books, 1981.

Brown, Lorraine, and John O'Conner, eds. *Free, Adult, Uncensored: The Living History of the Federal Theatre Project*. Washington: New Republic Books, 1978.

Brown, P., and S. Levinson. "Universals in Language Usage: Politeness Phenomena." In *Questions and Politeness: Strategies in Social Interaction*, edited by E. Goody, 56–289. Cambridge: Cambridge University Press, 1978.

Bruce, M. *The Making of Urban History: Historiography through Oral History*. Beverly Hills, CA: Sage Publications, 1977.

Bruley, Sue. *Socialism and Feminism in the Communist Party of Great Britain*. London: University of London, 1980.

Bruner, Jerome. "Life as Narrative." *Social Research* 54 (Spring 1987): 11–32.

Bruyn, S. T. *The Human Perspective in Sociology: The Methodology of Participant Observation*. Englewood Cliffs, NJ: Prentice-Hall, 1966.

Bruzzone, Anna Maria. "Women in Italian Resistance." In *Our Common History: The Transformation of Europe*, edited by Paul Thompson, 273–83. London: Pluto Press, 1982.

Bull, Edvard. "Industrial Boy Labour in Norway." In *Our Common History: The Transformation of Europe*, edited by Paul Thompson, 223–41. London: Pluto Press, 1982.

Burchard, Jorgen, and Carl Erik Andresen. "Oral History, People's Oral History and Social Change in Scandinavia." *Oral History* 8 (Autumn 1980): 25–29.

Burgess, R., ed. *Field Research: A Sourcebook and Field Manual.* London: Allen and Unwin, 1982.

Burke, Kenneth. *The Rhetoric of Religion.* Boston: Beacon Press, 1961.

Burleson, Joe W. Recorded interview by E. Culpepper Clark, 2 August 1978. Department of Speech Communication, University of Alabama.

Burman, Rickie. "The Jewish Woman as Breadwinner: The Changing Value of Women's Work in a Manchester Immigrant Community." *Oral History* 10 (Autumn 1982): 27–39.

Butler, Robert N. "The Life Review: An Interpretation of Reminiscence for the Aged." *Psychiatry* 26 (1963): 65–76.

Cannell, Charles F., Sally A. Lawson, and Doris L. Hausser. *A Technique for Evaluating Interviewer Performance.* Ann Arbor, MI: Survey Research Center of the Institute for Social Research, University of Michigan, 1975.

Cappella, J., and S. Planalp. "Talk and Silence Sequences in Informal Conversations III: Interspeaker Influence." *Human Communication Research* 7 (1981): 117–32.

Carter, Jan. *Nothing To Spare: Recollections of Australian Pioneering Women.* Sydney, Australia: Penguin, 1981.

Catani, Maurizio. "Social Life History as Ritualized Oral Exchange." In *Biography and Society*, edited by Daniel Bertaux, 211–22. Beverly Hills, CA: Sage Publications, 1981.

Chalasinski, Jozef. "The Life Records of the Young Generation of Polish Peasants as a Manifestation of Contemporary Culture." In *Biography and Society*, edited by Daniel Bertaux, 119–32. London: Sage Publications, 1981.

Chatman, Seymour. *Story and Discourse: Narrative Structure in Fiction and Film.* Ithaca, NY: Cornell University Press, 1978.

Christians, Clifford G., and James W. Carey. "The Logic and Aims of Qualitative Research." In *Research Methods in Mass Communication*, edited by Guido H. Stempel III, and Bruce H. Westley, 342–62. Englewood Cliffs, NJ: Prentice-Hall, 1981.

Christy, Marion. *Invasions of Privacy: Notes from a Celebrity Journalist*. Reading, MA: Addison-Wesley, 1984.

Cicourel, Aaron. *Cognitive Sociology: Language and Meaning in Social Interaction*. London: Cox and Wyman, 1973.

Clark, E. Culpepper, Michael J. Hyde, and Eva M. McMahan. "Communication in the Oral History Interview: Investigating Problems of Interpreting Oral Data." *International Journal of Oral History* 1 (February 1980): 28–40.

———. "Developing Instruction in Oral History: A New Avenue for Speech Communication." *Communication Education* 30 (July 1981): 237–44.

Clark, E. Culpepper. "The Oral History Interview." In *Effective Interviewing*, edited by Alexander Toler, 178–95. Springfield, IL: Charles C. Thomas, 1985.

Clarke, David D. *Language and Action: A Structural Model of Behavior*. New York: Pergamon Press, 1983.

Cohen, Cindy. "Building Multicultural and Intergenerational Networks through Oral History." *Frontiers* 7 (1983): 98–102.

Collett, P. "The Rules of Conduct." In *Social Rules and Social Behavior*, edited by P. Collett, 1–27. Totowa, NJ: Rowman and Littlefield, 1977.

Collingwood, R. G. *The Idea of History*. New York: Galaxy Books, 1956.

———. *An Autobiography*. London: Oxford University Press, 1939.

Colman, Gould P. "Oral History at Cornell." *Wilson Library Bulletin* 40 (1965–66): 624–28.

Cooke, Dick. "The Voice of an Immigrant into the South Wales Coalfield," recorded by Hywel Francis. *Oral History: The Journal of the Oral History Society* 9 (Autumn 1981): 41–48.

Cooper, Patricia, and Norma Bradley Buferd. *The Quilters: Women and Domestic Art, an Oral History*. Garden City, NY: Doubleday, 1978.

Cottle, Thomas J. *Private Lives and Public Accounts*. Amherst, MA: University of Massachusetts Press, 1977.

Couch, William T., ed. *These Are Our Lives*. Chapel Hill: University of North Caroina Press, 1939.

Coulmas, Florian, ed. *Conversational Routine*. The Hague: Mouton, 1981.

Coulthard, Malcolm, and Martin Montgomery, eds. *Studies in Discourse Analysis*. Boston: Routledge and Kegan Paul, 1981.

Cox, J. Robert, and Charles A. Willard, eds. *Advances in Argumentation Theory and Research*. Carbondale, IL: Southern Illinois University Press, 1983.

Craig, Robert T., and Karen Tracy, eds. *Conversational Coherence:*

Form, Structure, and Strategy. Beverly Hills, CA: Sage Publications, 1983.

Crook, Rosemary. "Tidy Women: Women in the Rhonda between the Wars." *Oral History* 10 (Autumn 1982): 40–46.

Davis, Cullom, Kathryn Back, and Kay MacLean. *Oral History From Tape to Type*. Chicago: American Library Association, 1977.

deCamargo, Aspasia A. "The Actor and the System: Trajectory of the Brazilian Political Elites." In *Biography and Society*, edited by Daniel Bertaux, 191–201. Beverly Hills, CA: Sage Publications, 1981.

Delia, Jesse, and Larry Grossberg. "Interpretation and Evidence." *Western Journal of Speech Communication* (Winter 1977): 32–42.

Denzin, Norman. "Introduction to Problems of Design and Analysis." In *Sociological Methods: A Sourcebook*, edited by Norman K. Denzin, 213–20. Chicago: Aldine, 1970.

———. "The Research Act." In *Symbolic Interaction: A Reader in Social Psychology*, edited by Jerome G. Manis and Bernard N. Meltzer, 58–68. Boston: Allyn and Bacon, 1978.

———. "The Interactionist Study of Social Organization: A Note On Method." In *Biography and Society*, edited by Daniel Bertaux, 149–67. Beverly Hills, CA: Sage Publications, 1981.

Dexter, Lewis Anthony. *Elite and Specialized Interviewing*. Evanston, IL: Northwestern University Press, 1970.

Diaz-Royo, Antonio. "Maneuvers and Transformations in Ethno-biographies of Puerto Rican Migrants." *International Journal of Oral History* 4 (1983): 19–28.

Disman, Milada. "Listening to Immigrants: From Memories and Narratives to Questions of Sociological Inquiry." *International Journal of Oral History* 6 (1985): 76–91.

Dolci, Danilo. *Sicilian Lives*. Translated by Justin Vitiello and Madeline Polidoro. New York: Pantheon Books, 1981.

Dos Passos, John. *The Ground We Stand on: Some Examples from the History of a Political Creed*. New York: Harcourt Brace, 1941.

Douglass, Dave. "Worms of the Earth." *New Statesman* 99 (21 March 1980): 434–37.

Downs, N. "Sir Walter Scott and Oral History." *Notes and Queries* 28 (August 1981): 321–22.

Drachnik, Joseph B. Recorded interview by William W. Moss, 27 July 1970. John F. Kennedy Library Oral History Program, Boston.

Dunaway, David K., and Willa K. Baum, eds. *Oral History: An Interdisciplinary Anthology*. Nashville: American Association for State and Local History, 1984.

Duncan, Hugh Dalziel. *Culture and Democracy: The Struggle for*

Form in Society and Architecture in Chicago and the Middle West during the Life and Times of Louis H. Sullivan. New York: Bedminster Press, 1965.

Duncan, Starkey, and Donald Fiske. *Face-to-Face Interaction: Research Methods and Theory*. Hillsdale, NJ: Lawrence Erlbaum, 1977.

Ebeling, G. *The Problem of Historicity in the Church and its Proclamation*. Philadelphia: Fortress Press, 1967.

Elder, Glen. "History and the Life Course." In *Biography and Society*, edited by Daniel Bertaux, 77–115. Beverly Hills, CA: Sage Publications, 1981.

Elegoet, Fanch. "The Peasant Economy of Leon, Brittany." In *Our Common History: The Transformation of Europe*, edited by Paul Thompson, 111–23. London: Pluto Press, 1982.

Ellis, Donald G., M. Hamilton, and L. Aho. "Some Issues in Conversational Coherence." *Human Communication Research* 9 (1983): 267–82.

Ellis, Donald G., and William A. Donohue, eds. *Contemporary Issues in Language and Discourse Processes*. Hillsdale, NJ: Lawrence Erlbaum, 1986.

Ellul, Jacques. *Propaganda*. Translated by Konrad Kellen. New York: Alfred A. Knopf, 1965.

Ellwood, David, and Anna Bravo. "Oral History and Resistance History in Italy." In *Our Common History: The Transformation of Europe*, edited by Paul Thompson, 284–96. London: Pluto Press, 1982.

Falford, Robert. "People Will Talk: Oral History Is Dramatic, Democratic, and Immensely Popular, But Is It a Valid Depiction of the Past?" *Saturday Night* 96 (October 1981): 5–6.

Farrell, Edmund J. "Oral Histories as Living Literature." *English Journal* 71 (April 1982): 87–92.

Felman, Shoshana. *The Literary Speech Act*. Ithaca, NY: Cornell University Press, 1983.

Ferrarott, Franco. "On the Autonomy of the Biographical Method." In *Biography and Society*, edited by Daniel Bertaux, 19–27. London: Sage Publications, 1981.

Fielding, Nigel G., and Jane L. Fielding. *Linking Data*. Beverly Hills, CA: Sage Publications, 1986.

Fischer, Lucy Rose. "Sociology and Life History: Methodological Incongruence?" *International Journal of Oral History* 4 (February 1983): 29–40.

Fixico, Donald. Review of *Nations Remembered: An Oral History of the Five Civilized Tribes 1865–1907*, by Theda Purdue. *Inter-*

national *Journal of Oral History* 2 (1981): 221–23.

Foner, Eric, comp. *America's Black Past: A Reader in Afro-American History*. New York: Harper and Row, 1970.

Foronda, Marcelino A., Jr. "Oral History in the Phillipines: Trends and Prospects." *International Journal of Oral History* 2 (1981): 13–25.

Fox, Daniel M. "The Achievement of the Federal Writers' Project." *American Quarterly* 13, no. 1 (1961): 3–19.

Francis, Hywel. "The Background and Motives of Welsh Volunteers in the International Brigades, 1936–1938." *International Journal of Oral History* 2 (1981): 84–100.

———. *Miners Against Fascism: Wales and the Spanish Civil War*. London: Lawrence and Wishart, 1984.

Francis, Hywel, and David Smith. *The Fed: A History of the South Wales Miners in the Twentieth Century*. London: Lawrence and Wishart, 1980.

Frelinghysen, Peter H. B. Recorded interviews by Ronald J. Grele, 7 June 1966 and 29 September 1978, New Jersey Historical Commission Oral History Program.

Friedlander, Peter. *The Emergence of a UAW Local, 1936–1939: A Study in Class and Culture*. Pittsburgh: University of Pittsburgh Press, 1975.

Frisch, Michael. "Oral History and Hard Times: A Review Essay." *The Oral History Review* (1979): 70–79.

Gadamer, Hans-Georg. *Truth and Method*. Edited by Garrett Borden and John Cumming. New York: Continuum, 1975.

———. *Philosophical Hermeneutics*. Edited and translated by David E. Linge. Berkeley: University of California Press, 1976.

———. *Being and Time*. Translated by John McQuarrie and Edward Robinson. London: SCM Press, 1962.

Gagron, Nicole. "On the Analysis of Life Accounts." In *Biography and Society*, edited by Daniel Bertaux, 47–60. Beverly Hills, CA: Sage Publications, 1981.

Gallagher, Dorothy. *Hannah's Daughters: Six Generations of an American Family, 1876–1976*. New York: Thomas Crowell, 1976.

Gallie, W. B. *Philosophy and the Historical Understanding*. New York: Schocken Books, 1964.

Ganz, Joan S. *Rules: A Systematic Study*. The Hague: Mouton, 1971.

Garrett, Annette. *Interviewing: Its Principles and Methods*. New York: Family Service Association of America, 1970.

Geertz, Clifford. *The Interpretation of Culture*. New York: Basic Books, 1973.

————. *Local Knowledge: Further Essays in Interpretive Anthropology.* New York: Basic Books, 1983.

Georges, Robert A., and Michael O. Jones. *People Studying People: The Human Element in Fieldwork.* Berkeley, CA: University of California Press, 1980.

Gittins, Diana. "Let the People Speak: Oral History in Britain." *Victorian Studies* 26 (Summer 1983): 431–41.

Glaser, Barney, and Anselm Strauss. *Discovery of Grounded Theory.* Chicago: Aldine, 1967.

Glassie, Henry. *Passing the Time in Ballymenone.* Philadelphia: University of Pennsylvania Press, 1982.

————. *Irish Folk History: Texts from the North.* Philadelphia: University of Pennsylvania Press, 1982.

Gluck, Sherna. *From Parlor to Prison: Five American Suffragettes Talk about Their Lives.* New York: Vintage Press, 1976.

Goffman, Erving. *Strategic Interaction.* Philadelphia: University of Pennsylvania Press, 1969.

Goldman, Harry M. "Workers Theatre to Broadway Hit: The Evolution of an American Radical Revue." *Oral History: The Journal of the Oral History Society* 10 (Spring 1982): 56–66.

Goodwin, Charles. *Conversational Organization.* New York: Academic Press, 1981.

Goodwin, M. H. " 'Instigating': Storytelling as Social Process." *American Ethnologist* 9 (1982): 799–819.

Gorden, Raymond L. *Interviewing: Strategy, Techniques and Tactics.* Rev. ed. Homewood, IL: Dorsey Press, 1969.

Gottdiener, M. "Field Research and Videotape." *Sociological Inquiry* 49 (1980): 59–66.

Gottschalk, Louis, Clyde Kluckhohn, and Robert Angell. *The Use of Personal Documents in History, Anthropology, and Sociology.* Social Science Research Council, Bulletin no. 53. New York, 1945.

Gough, Richard. *The History of Myddle.* Middlesex, England: Penguin Books, 1980.

Goulborne, Harry. "Oral History and Black Labour in Britain: An Overview." *Oral History* 8 (Spring 1980): 24–34.

Graham, Stanley. "The Lancashire Textile Project: A Description of the Work and Some of the Techniques Involved." *Oral History* 8 (Autumn 1980): 48–52.

Grele, Ronald J., ed. *Envelopes of Sound: Six Practitioners Discuss the Method, Theory and Practice of Oral History and Oral Testimony.* Chicago: Precedent Publishing, 1975.

————. "Movement without Aim: Methodological and Theoretical Problems in Oral History." In *Envelopes of Sound: The Art of*

Oral History, 2d ed., edited by Ronald J. Grele, 126–54. Chicago: Precedent Publishing, 1985.

———. "Private Memories and Public Presentation: The Art of Oral History." In *Envelopes of Sound: The Art of Oral History*, ed. Ronald J. Grele, 242–83. Chicago: Precedent Publishing, 1985.

———. "Can Anyone Over Thirty Be Trusted? A Friendly Critique of Oral History." In *Envelopes of Sound: The Art of Oral History*, ed. Ronald J. Grele, 196–210. Chicago: Precedent Publishing, 1985.

———. "A Surmisable Variety: Interdisciplinarity and Oral History." In *Envelopes of Sound: The Art of Oral History*, ed. Ronald J. Grele, 156–95. Chicago: Precedent Publishing, 1985.

Grice, H. P. "Logic and Conversation." In *Syntax and Semantics*. Vol. 3, *Speech Acts*. Edited by P. Cole and J. L. Morgan, 41–58. New York: Academic Press, 1975.

Grossberg, Lawrence. "Dialectical Hermeneutics and the Human Sciences: Foundations for a Cultural Approach to Communication." Ph.D. diss., University of Illinois, 1976.

Grossman, Vasily, and Illya Ehrenburg, eds. *The Black Book*. Translated by John Glad. New York: Holocaust Library/Shocken Books, 1982.

Gumperz, John J. *Discourse Strategies*. New York: Cambridge University Press, 1982.

Gumperz, John J., and D. Hymes, eds. *Directions in Sociolinguistics*. New York: Holt, Rinehart, and Winston, 1972.

Gumperz, John J., ed. *Language and Social Identity*. New York: Cambridge University Press, 1982.

Gwaltney, John Langston. *Drylongso: A Self Portrait of Black America*. New York: Random House, 1980.

Habermas, Jurgen. *Knowledge and Human Interests*. Translated by Jeremy J. Shapiro. Boston: Beacon Press, 1971.

Hall, Stuart, ed. *Culture, Media, and Language*. London: Hutchinson, 1980.

Hamilton, Sheila. "Interviewing the Middle Class: Women Graduates of the Scottish Universities, c. 1910–1935." *Oral History* 10 (Autumn 1982): 58–67.

Hankiss, Agnes. "Ontologies of the Self: On the Mythological Rearranging of One's Life History." In *Biography and Society*, edited by Daniel Bertaux, 203–9. Beverly Hills, CA: Sage Publications, 1981.

Hareven, Tamara K. *Amoskeag: Life and Work in an American Factory City*. New York: Pantheon Books, 1978.

Harre, Roman. "Some Remarks on 'Rule' as a Scientific Concept." In *Understanding Other Persons*, edited by Theodore Mischel, 143–84. Totowa, NJ: Rowman and Littlefield, 1974.

————. "The Ethogenic Approach: Theory and Practice." In *Advances in Experimental Social Psychology*, Vol. 10, edited by Leonard Berkowitz, 283–314. New York: Academic Press, 1977.

————. *Social Being: A Theory for Social Psychology*. Totowa, NJ: Rowman and Littlefield, 1979.

Harre, Roman, and Paul Secord. *The Explanation of Social Behavior*. Oxford: Basil Blackwell, 1972.

Harris, Alice Kessler. "Introduction." In *Envelopes of Sound: The Art of Oral History*, edited by Ronald J. Grele, 6–7. Chicago: Precedent Publishing, 1985.

Hay, Cynthia. "The Pangs of the Past." *Oral History* 9 (Spring 1983): 41–46.

Heidegger, Martin. *Being and Time*. Translated by John Macquarrie and Edward Robinson. New York: Harper and Row, 1962.

Heinz, Luther C. Recorded interviews by William W. Moss, 20 and 27 July 1970. John F. Kennedy Library Oral History Program.

Henige, David. *Oral Historiography*. London: Longman, 1982.

Hentoff, Nat, and Nat Shapiro, eds. *Hear Me Talkin to Ya: The Story of Jazz as Told by the Men Who Made It*. 1955. Reprint. New York: Dover Publications, 1966.

Heritage, John. "Analyzing News Interviews: Aspects of the Production of Talk for an Overhearing Audience." In *Handbook of Discourse Analysis*, edited by Teun Van Dijk, 95–119. London: Academic Press, 1985.

Herrmann, T. *Speech and Situation: A Psychological Conception of Situation Speaking*. New York: Springer-Verlag, 1983.

Hexter, J. H. *Doing History*. London: George Allen and Unwin, 1971.

Hirsch, E. D., Jr. *Validity in Interpretation*. New Haven: Yale University Press, 1967.

————. *The Aims of Interpretation*. Chicago: University of Chicago Press, 1976.

Hoff, Rhoda. *America's Immigrants: Adventures in Eyewitness History*. New York: H. Z. Walck, 1967.

Holden, Len. "Think of Me Simply as the Skipper: Industrial Relations at Vauxhall's, 1920–1950." *Oral History: Journal of the Oral History Society* 9 (Autumn 1981): 19–32.

Hoopes, James. *Oral History: An Introduction for Students*. Chapel Hill: University of North Carolina Press, 1979.

Hopper, R. "The 'Taken-For-Granted'." *Human Communication Research* 7 (1981): 195–211.

Howe, Irving. *World of Our Fathers*. New York: Harcourt Brace and Jovanovich, 1976.

Howell, William. Recorded interview by Ronald J. Grele, 4 February 1970. New Jersey Historical Commission Oral History Program.

Howells, Kim, and Merfyn Jones. "Oral History and Contemporary History." *Oral History* 11 (Autumn 1983): 15–20.

Howerth, Ken. "The North West Sound Archive: An Interdisciplinary Venture." *Museum's Journal* 81 (September 1981): 99–102.

Hoy, David Couzens. *The Critical Circle: Literature, History, and Philosophical Hermeneutics.* Berkeley: University of California Press, 1978.

Humphreys, Hubert D. "Oral History Research in Louisiana: An Overview." *Louisiana History* 20 (1979): 353–71.

———. "Oral History: An Overview." In *A Guide to the History of Louisiana,* edited by Light Townsend Cummins and Glen Jeansonne, 103–13. Westport, CT: Greenwood Press, 1982.

Hyde, Michael J. "On the Reifying Tendency and the Liberating Functions of Speech." *Eros* 7 (1980): 54–81.

———. "Philosophical Hermeneutics and the Communicative Experience: The Paradigm of Oral History." *Man and World* 13 (1980): 81–98.

Ihde, Don, ed. *The Conflict of Interpretations, Essays in Hermeneutics.* Evanston, IL: Northwestern University Press, 1974.

Ives, Edward D. *The Tape-Recorded Interview: A Manual for Field Workers in Folklore and Oral History.* Knoxville: University of Tennessee Press, 1980.

Ivey, Allen E. *Intentional Interviewing and Counseling.* Belmont, CA: Wadsworth, 1983.

Jackson, Bruce. *Fieldwork.* Urbana, IL: University of Illinois Press, 1987.

Jackson, Sally, and Scott Jacobs. "Structure of Conversational Argument: Pragmatic Bases for the Enthymeme." *Quarterly Journal of Speech* 66 (1980): 251–65.

———. "The Collaborative Production of Proposals in Conversational Argument and Persuasion: A Study in Disagreement Regulation." *Journal of the American Forensic Association* 18 (1981): 77–90.

Jacobs, Scott, and Sally Jackson. "Conversational Argument: A Discourse Analytic Approach." In *Advances in Argumentation Theory and Research,* edited by J. Robert Cox and Charles A. Willard, 205–37. Carbondale, IL: Southern Illinois University Press, 1983.

———. "Speech Act Structure in Conversation: Rational Aspects of Pragmatic Coherence." In *Conversational Coherence: Form, Structure, and Strategy,* edited by Robert T. Craig and Karen Tracy, 47–66. Beverly Hills, CA: Sage Publications, 1983.

Jalla, Daniele. "The Working Class Family in Turin: Traditional Values and the Economy." In *Our Common History: The Trans-*

formation of Europe, edited by Paul Thompson, 213–21. London: Pluto Press, 1982.

Jameson, Elizabeth, and David Lenfest, eds. "From Oral to Visual: A First-Timer's Introduction to Media Production." *Frontiers* 7 (1983): 25–31.

Jefferson, Gail. "Sequential Aspects of Storytelling in Conversation." In *Studies in the Organization of Conversational Interaction,* edited by Jim Schenkein, 219–48. New York: Academic Press, 1978.

Jellison, Charles A. *Tomatoes Were Cheaper: Tales from the Thirties.* Syracuse: Syracuse University Press, 1977.

John, Angela V. "Scratching the Surface: Women, Work and Coalmining History in England and Wales." *Oral History* 10 (Autumn 1982): 13–26.

Johnson, Douglas V. Recorded interview by William W. Moss, 13 July 1970. John F. Kennedy Library Oral History Program, Boston.

Jolly, Brad. *Videotaping Local History.* Nashville: American Association for State and Local History, 1982.

Jonas, Hans. "Change and Permanence: On the Possibility of Understanding History." *Social Research* 38 (1971): 498–528.

Jones, Howard Palfrey. Recorded interview by Dennis O'Brien, 23 June 1969. John F. Kennedy Library Oral History Program, Boston.

Jones, Merfyn. "Welsh Immigrants in the Cities of North West England, 1890–1930: Some Oral Testimony." *Oral History: The Journal of the Oral History Society* 9 (Autumn 1981): 33–41.

Joseph, Peter. *Good Times: An Oral History of America in the Nineteen-Sixties.* New York: William Morrow, 1974.

Josey, E. J., and Ann Allen Shockley, eds. *Handbook of Black Librarianship.* Littleton, CO: Libraries Unlimited, 1977.

Joshi, Aravind K., Bonnie L. Webber, and Ivan A. Sag, eds. *Elements of Discourse Understanding.* Cambridge: Cambridge University Press, 1981.

Joutard, Philippe. "A Regional Project: Ethnotexts." *Oral History* 9 (Spring 1981): 47–51.

Joyner, Charles W. "Oral History as Communicative Event: A Folkloristic Perspective." *Oral History Review* 7 (1979): 47–52.

Jurick, Donna. "The Enactment of Returning: A Naturalistic Study of Talk." *Communication Quarterly* 25 (Summer 1977): 21–29.

Kahn, Kathy. *Hillbilly Women.* New York: Doubleday, 1972.

Kaplan, Charles D. "Addict Life Stories: An Explanation of the Methodological Grounds for the Study of Social Problems, Part I." *International Journal of Oral History* 3 (February 1982): 31–50.

———. "Addict Life Stories: An Exploration of the Methodological

Grounds for the Study of Social Problems, Part II." *International Journal of Oral History* 3 (June 1982): 114–28.

Karpati, Zoltan. "The Methodological Use of the Life History Approach in a Hungarian Survey on Mobility and Urbanization." In *Biography and Society*, edited by Daniel Bertaux, 133–48. Beverly Hills, CA: Sage Publications, 1981.

Kearns, Doris. *Lyndon Johnson and the American Dream*. New York: Harper and Row, 1976.

Kearns, John T. *Using Language: The Structures of Speech Acts*. Albany: State University of New York Press, 1984.

Kelly, Jim. "An Interview with Ronald Fraser." *Oral History* 8 (Spring 1980): 52–57.

Kennedy, Liam. "Recent Development in Oral History in Northern Ireland." *Oral History: The Journal of the Oral History Society* 10 (Spring 1982): 14–17.

Kent, Allen, Harold Lancour, and Jay E. Daily, eds. *Encyclopedia of Library and Information Science*. New York: Marcel Dekker, 1977.

Key, Betty McKeever. "Oral History in the Library." *Catholic Library World* 49 (1978): 381–84.

———. "Publishing Oral History: Observations and Objections." *Oral History Review* 10 (1982): 145–52.

Kielman, Chester V. "The Texas Oil Industry Project." *Wilson Library Bulletin* 40 (1965–66): 616–18.

Kirk, Jerome, and Marc L. Miller. *Reliability and Validity in Qualitative Research*. Beverly Hills, CA: Sage Publications, 1986.

Klein-Andreu, Flora, ed. *Discourse Perspectives on Syntax*. New York: Academic Press, 1983.

Kockelmans, Joseph. "Towards an Interpretative or Hermeneutic Social Science." *New School for Social Science Research Graduate Faculty Philosophy Journal* 5 (Fall 1975): 73–96.

Koestler, Arthur. *The Ghost in the Machine*. Chicago: Henry Regnery, 1967.

Kohli, Martin. "Biography: Account, Text, Method." In *Biography and Society*, edited by Daniel Bertaux, 61–75. Beverly Hills, CA: Sage Publications, 1981.

Kramarae, Charles, Muriel Schultz, and William M. O'Barr. *Language and Power*. Beverly Hills, CA: Sage Publications, 1984.

Kroeber-Quinn, Theodora. "Retrospective on Oral History." *Oral History Review* 11 (1983): 103–8.

Labov, William, and David Fanshel. *Therapeutic Discourse*. New York: Academic Press, 1977.

Labov, William, and Joshua Waletsky. "Narrative Analysis: Oral Versions of Personal Experience." In *Essays on the Verbal and*

Visual Arts, edited by June Helm, 12–44. *Proceedings of the 1966 Annual Spring Meeting of the American Ethnological Society*. Seattle: American Ethnological Society, 1967.

Lance, David. "Oral History Archives: Perceptions and Practices." *Oral History* 8 (Autumn 1980): 59–63.

Langlois, W. J., ed. *A Guide to Aural History Research*. Victoria, BC: Aural History, Provincial Archives of Canada, 1976.

Lantz, Herman R. "Family and Kin as Revealed in the Narratives of Ex-Slaves." *Social Science Quarterly* 60 (March 1980): 667–75.

Lanzardo, Liliana. "Class Consciousness and the Fiat Workers of Turin Since 1943." In *Our Common History: The Transformation of Europe*, edited by Paul Thompson, 79–89. London: Pluto Press, 1982.

Levinson, S. *Pragmatics*. Cambridge: Cambridge University Press, 1983.

Lewis, Oscar. *The Children of Sanchez: Autobiography of a Mexican Family*. New York: Random House, 1961.

Lichtman, Allen J. *Your Family History: How To Use Oral History, Family Archives, and Public Documents To Discover Your Heritage*. New York: Vintage Books, 1978.

Lindquist, Sven. "Dig Where You Stand." In *Our Common History: The Transformation of Europe*, edited by Paul Thompson, 322–30. London: Pluto Press, 1982.

Lisagor, Peter. Recorded interview by Ronald J. Grele, 22 April 1966. John F. Kennedy Library Oral History Program, Boston.

Litton-Hawes, Elaine M. "A Discourse Analysis of Topic Co-Selection in Medical Interviews." Ph.D. diss., Department of Speech Communication, Ohio State University, 1976.

Lofgren, Orvar. "The Swedish Family: A Study of Privatisation and Social Change since 1880." In *Our Common History: The Transformation of Europe*, edited by Paul Thompson, 233–48. London: Pluto Press, 1982.

Longacre, Robert E. *The Grammar of Discourse*. New York: Plenum Press, 1983.

Luchterhand, Elmer. "Knowing and Not Knowing: Involvement in Nazi Genocide." In *Our Common History: The Transformation of Europe*, edited by Paul Thompson, 251–72. London: Pluto Press, 1982.

Luchterhand, Elmer, and Norbert Wieland. "The Focused Life History in Studying Involvement in a Genocidal Situation in Nazi Germany." In *Biography and Society*, edited by Daniel Bertaux, 267–88. Beverly Hills, CA: Sage Publications, 1981.

Lummis, Trevor. "Structure and Validity in Oral Evidence." *International Journal of Oral History* 2 (1981): 109–20.

Lynd, Alice, and Staughton Lynd. *Rank and File: Personal Histories of Working Class Organizers.* Boston: Beacon Press, 1973.

McDonald, William F. *The Federal Relief Administration and the Arts: The Origins and Administrative History of the Arts Project of the Works Progress Administration.* Columbus, OH: Ohio State University Press, 1969.

McLaughlin, Margaret L. *Conversation: How Talk Is Organized.* Beverly Hills, CA: Sage Publications, 1984.

McMahan, Eva M. "Communicative Dynamics of Hermeneutical Conversation in Oral History Interviews." *Communication Quarterly* 31 (Winter 1983): 3–11.

———. "Speech and Counterspeech: Language-In-Use in Oral History Fieldwork." *Oral History Review* 15 (Spring 1987): 185–208.

McNulty, Anne, and Hilary Troop. *Directory of the British Oral History Collection,* Vol. 1. Colchester, England: The Oral History Society, University of Sussex, 1982.

McPherson, Marion White. "Some Values and Limitations of Oral Histories." *Journal of the History of the Behavioral Sciences* 11 (January 1975): 34–36.

McWilliams, Jerry. *The Preservation and Restoration of Sound Recordings.* Nashville: American Association for State and Local History, 1979.

Maccoby, Eleanor E., and Nathan Maccoby. "The Interview: A Tool of Social Science." In *The Handbook of Social Psychology,* Vol. 1, edited by Gardner Lindzey, 449–87. Cambridge, MA: Addison-Wesley, 1954.

Mackay, Margaret. "Nineteenth Century Tirce Emigrant Communities in Ontario." *Oral History: The Journal of the Oral History Society* 9 (Autumn 1981): 49–60.

Macleod, Dawn. "Scenes of the Near Past: Born in the Stone." *Blackwood's Magazine* (June 1980): 430–41.

Mahler, Walter R. *How Effective Executives Interview.* Homewood, IL: Dow Jones-Irwin, 1976.

Mangione, Jerre. *The Dream and the Deal: The Federal Writer's Project 1935–1943.* Boston: Little, Brown, 1972.

Maple, Frank F. *Shared Decision Making.* Beverly Hills, CA: Sage Publications, 1977.

Mason, Elizabeth B., and Louis M. Starr, eds. *The Oral History Collection of Columbia University.* New York: Oral History and Research Office, Columbia University, 1979.

Mason, Elizabeth B. "An Introduction to Oral History." *Maryland Historian* 13 (1982): 1–2.

Mason, Michael, Basil Greenhill, and Robin Craig. *The British Seafarer.* London: Hutchinson, 1980.

Matson, Floyd W. *The Broken Image: Man, Science and Society.* Garden City, NY: Doubleday, 1966.

Mayhew, Henry. *London Labour and the London Poor.* London, 1861. Reprint. New York: Penguin, 1968.

Mead, George Herbert. *Mind, Self and Society.* Edited by Charles W. Morris. Chicago: University of Chicago Press, 1934.

Meckler, Alan, and Ruth McMullin, comps. *Oral History Collections.* New York: R. R. Bowker, 1975.

Millar, David. "Ordinary People, Extraordinary History." *Canadian Oral History Association Journal* 5 (1981–82): 19–24.

Miller, Jonathan. *Marshall McLuhan.* New York: Viking Press, 1971.

Miller, Joseph C., ed. *The African Past Speaks: Essays on Oral Tradition and History.* London: William Dawson and Sons, 1980.

Miller, Merle. *Lyndon: An Oral Biography.* New York: Putnam, 1980.

Mink, Louis. "The Anatomy of Historical Understanding." *History and Theory* 5 (1965): 24–47.

Mintz, Sidney W. "The Anthropological Interview and the Life History." *Oral History Review* 7 (1979): 18–26.

Mishler, Elliot G. *Research Interviewing: Context and Narrative.* Cambridge, MA: Harvard University Press, 1986.

Misztal, Bronislaw. "Autobiographies, Diaries, Life Histories, and Oral Histories of Workers as a Source of Socio-Historical Knowledge." *International Journal of Oral History* 2 (1981): 181–94.

Mitchell, David J. "Living Documents: Oral History and Biography." *Oral History and Biography* 3 (1980): 283–95.

Mitchell, W. J. T., ed. *On Narrative.* Chicago: University of Chicago Press, 1981.

Modell, Judith. "Stories and Strategies: The Use of Personal Statements." *International Journal of Oral History* 4 (February 1983): 4–11.

Moerman, Michael. *Talking Culture: Ethnography and Conversation Analysis.* Philadelphia: University of Pennsylvania Press, 1987.

Mohan, B. A. "Do Sequencing Rules Exist?" *Semiotica* 12 (1974): 75–96.

Morantz, Regina Markell, Cynthia Stodola Pomerleau, and Carol Hansen Fenichel. *In Her Own Words: Oral Histories of Women Physicians.* Westport, CT: Greenwood Press, 1982.

Morin, Francoise. "Anthropological *Praxis* and Life History." Translated by Kathleen Heffron. *International Journal of Oral History* 3 (February 1982): 5–30.

Morrissette, Bruce. *Novel and Film: Essays in Two Genres.* Chicago: University of Chicago Press, 1985.

Morrissey, Charles T. "Oral History: More than Tapes Are Spinning." *Library Journal* 105 (15 April 1980): 932–33.

―――. "The Imprint of History on Life-Course Research: Oral History and the Berkeley Guidance Study." *International Journal of Oral History* 3 (February 1982): 51–63.

―――. "John Hawkes on Tape: The Paradox of Self-Identity in a Recorded Interview." *International Journal of Oral History* 6 (1985): 47–56.

Moss, William W. *Oral History Program Manual.* New York: Praeger Publishing, 1974.

―――. "Oral History: An Appreciation." *The American Archivist* 40 (October 1977): 429–39.

―――. "In Search of Values." *Oral History Review* 7 (1979): 1–5.

Murray, James Briggs. "Oral History/Video Documentation at the Schomburg Center: More than Just 'Talking Heads.' " *Film Library Quarterly* 15 (1982): 23–27.

Namias, June. *First Generation: Oral Histories of Twentieth-Century American Immigrants.* Boston: Beacon Press, 1978.

Neuenschwander, John A. *Oral History as a Teaching Approach.* Washington: NEA, 1976.

―――. "Remembrance of Things Past: Oral Historians and Long-Term Memory." *Oral History Review* (1978): 45–53.

Nevins, Allen. "Oral History: How and Why It Was Born." *Wilson Library Bulletin* 40 (1965–66): 600–601.

Newbury, Maggie. *Reminiscences of a Bradford Mill Girl.* Bradford, England: City of Bradford Local Studies Library, 1980.

Newman, Dale. "Culture, Class and Christianity in a Cotton Mill Village." *Oral History* 8 (Autumn 1980): 36–47.

Niblett, Chris. "Oral Testimony and the Social History of Technology." *Oral History* 8 (Autumn 1980): 53–57.

Niethammer, Lutz. "Oral History as a Channel of Communication Between Workers and Historians." In *Our Common History: The Transformation of Europe,* edited by Paul Thompson, 23–37. London: Pluto Press, 1982.

Nofsinger, Robert E., Jr. "On Answering Questions Indirectly: Some Rules in the Grammar of Doing Conversation." *Human Communication Research* 2 (1976): 172–81.

―――. "A Peek at Conversational Analysis." *Communication Quarterly* 25 (Summer 1977): 12–20.

O'Keefe, Barbara, and Jesse G. Delia. "Psychological and Interactional Dimensions of Communicative Development." In *Recent Advances in Language, Communication and Social Psychology,* edited by H. Giles and R. St. Clair, 41–85. London: Lawrence Erlbaum, 1985.

O'Keefe, Daniel J. "Two Concepts of Argument." *The Journal of the American Forensic Association* 13 (Winter 1977): 123–28.

Olson, Alan M., ed. *Myth, Symbol and Reality*. Notre Dame: University of Notre Dame Press, 1980.

Olson, Mary, and Barbara A. Hatcher. "Cultural Journalism: A Bridge to the Past." *Education Digest* 47 (May 1982): 46–48.

Owen, Marion. *Apologies and Remedial Interchanges: A Study of Language Use in Social Interaction*. New York: Mouton, 1983.

Pakenham, Thomas. "The Comprehension of Private Cooper." *Oral History: The Journal of the Oral History Society* 9 (Autumn 1981): 61–66.

Palmer, R. E. *Hermeneutics: Interpretation Theory in Schleiermacher, Dilthey, Heidegger, and Gadamer*. Evanston, IL: Northwestern University Press, 1969.

Palmer, Roy. "A Tribute to Charles Parker." *Oral History: The Journal of the Oral History Society* 10 (Spring 1982): 12.

Passerini, Luisa. "Work Ideology and Working Class Attitudes to Fascism." In *Our Common History: The Transformation of Europe*, edited by Paul Thompson, 54–78. London: Pluto Press, 1982.

Pearce, W. Barnett, Vernon E. Cronen, and Linda M. Harris. "Methodological Considerations in Building Human Communication Theory." In *Human Communication Theory*, edited by Frank E. X. Dance, 1–43. New York: Harper and Row, 1982.

Pecheux, Michel. *Language, Semantics and Ideology: Stating the Obvious*. London: Macmillan, 1982.

Pells, Richard H. *Radical Visions and American Dreams: Culture and Social Thought in the Depression Years*. New York: Harper and Row, 1974.

Penkower, Monty Noam. *The Federal Writer's Project: A Study in Government Patronage of the Arts*. Urbana, IL: University of Illinois Press, 1977.

Perdue, Charles. *Weevils in the Wheat: Interviews with Virginia Ex-Slaves*. Charlottesville: University of Virginia Press, 1976.

Perdue, Theda. *Nations Remembered: An Oral History of the Five Civilized Tribes 1865–1907*. London, England: Greenwood Press, 1980.

Pfaff, Eugene, Jr. "Oral History: A New Challenge for Public Libraries." *Wilson Library Bulletin* 54 (1980): 568–71.

Plummer, Ken. *Documents of Life: An Introduction to the Problems and Literature of a Humanistic Method*. London: George Allen and Unwin, 1983.

Pogue, Forrest C. "The George C. Marshall Oral-History Project." *Wilson Library Bulletin* 40 (1965–66): 607–08, 613–15.

Polansky, Norman A. "How Shall A Life-History Be Written?" *Journal of Personality* 9 (1941): 188–207.

Polanyi, Livia. "Conversational Storytelling." In *Handbook of Discourse Analysis*, Vol. 3, edited by Teun van Dijk, 183–201. London: Academic Press, 1985.

Pomerantz, Anita. "Agreeing and Disagreeing with Assessments: Some Features of Preferred/Dispreferred Turn Shapes." In *Structures of Social Action*, edited by J. Atkinson and J. Heritage, 57–101. Cambridge: Cambridge University Press, 1984.

Portelli, Alessandro. "The Time of My Life: Functions of Time in Oral History." *International Journal of Oral History* 2 (1981): 162–80.

Pratt, Mary Louise. *Toward a Speech Act Theory of Literary Discourse*. Bloomington, IN: Indiana University Press, 1977.

Prince, Gerald. *Narratology: The Form and Functioning of Narrative*. New York: Mouton, 1982.

Psathas, G., ed. *Everyday Language*. New York: Irvington, 1979.

Punch, Maurice. *The Politics and Ethics of Fieldwork*. Beverly Hills, CA: Sage Publications, 1986.

Rawick, George P. *The American Slave: A Composite Autobiography*, Vol. 1: *From Sundown to Sunup; The Making of the Black Community*. Westport, CT: Greenwood Publishing, 1972.

Reardon, K. K. "Conversational Deviance: A Structural Model." *Human Communication Research* 9 (1982): 59–74.

Reid, David. "Full of Noises." *New Library World* 81 (August 1980): 155–56.

Reimer, Derek, and Jean Dryden. "Oral History and Archives: The Case in Favor." *Canadian Oral History Association Journal* 5 (1981–82): 30–37.

Renvoize, Jean. *Incest: A Family Pattern*. London: Routledge and Kegan Paul, 1983.

Reuss, Henry S. Recorded interview by Ronald J. Grele, 12 and 15 December 1965. John F. Kennedy Library Oral History Program, Boston.

Reynolds, Paul. *A Primer in Theory Construction*. Indianapolis: Bobbs-Merrill, 1971.

Richards, Sam. "Bill Hingston—A Biography in Song." *Oral History: The Journal of the Oral History Society* 10 (Spring 1982): 24–46.

Richardson, Stephen A., Barbara S. Dohrenwend, and David Klein. *Interviewing: Its Forms and Functions*. New York: Basic Books, 1965.

Ricoeur, Paul. "The Model of the Text: Meaningful Action Considered as a Text." *New Literary History* 5 (1973): 91–117.

————. *Interpretation Theory: Discourse and the Surplus of Meaning.* Fort Worth: Texas Christian University Press, 1976.

Robertson, Jean Ellis. *Language in Oral Histories: The Shape of Discourse about the Past.* Ph.D. diss., University of Pennsylvania, 1983.

Robinson, John A. "Personal Narratives Reconsidered." *Journal of American Folklore* 94 (1981): 58–85.

Rommetveit, R. *On Message Structure: A Framework for the Study of Language and Communication.* London: John Wiley and Sons, 1974.

Rosaldo, Renato. "Doing Oral History." *Social Analysis* 4 (1980): 89–99.

Rosenzweig, Roy. "Automating Your Oral History Program: A Guide to Data Base Management on a Microcomputer." *International Journal of Oral History* 5 (1984): 174–87.

Ross, Ellen. Review of *East Underworld*, Vol. 3: *Chapters in the Life of Arthur Harding*, by Ralph Samuel. *International Journal of Oral History* 4 (1983): 130–33.

Ross, Martha. "Interviewer or Intervener: Interpretation in the Oral History Interview." *Maryland Historian* 13 (1982): 3–6.

Royal, Robert F., and Steven R. Schutt. *The Gentle Art of Interviewing and Interrogation: A Professional Manual and Guide.* Englewood Cliffs, NJ: Prentice-Hall, 1976.

Rumics, Elizabeth. "Oral History: Defining the Term." *Wilson Library Bulletin* 40 (1965–66): 602–5.

Ryant, Carl. "Oral History as Popular Culture." *Journal of Popular Culture* 15 (Spring 1982): 60–66.

Sacks, Harvey. "On the Analysability of Stories by Children." In *Directions in Sociolinguistics*, edited by J. Gumperz and D. Hymes, 325–45. New York: Holt, Rinehart and Winston, 1972.

————. "An Initial Investigation of the Usability of Conversational Data for Doing Sociology." In *Studies in Social Interaction*, edited by David Sudnow, 31–74. New York: Free Press, 1972.

Samuel, Raphael. *East Underworld*, Vol. 2: *Chapters in the Life of Arthur Harding.* London and Boston: Routledge and Kegan Paul, 1981.

Sanders, Marion K., and Saul Alinsky. *The Professional Radical: Conversations with Saul Alinsky.* New York: Harper and Row, 1970.

Santoli, Albert. *Everything We Had: An Oral History of the Vietnam War by Thirty-Three American Soldiers Who Fought It.* New York: Random House, 1981.

Schegloff, Emmanuel. "Sequencing in Conversational Openings." In

Directions in Sociolinguistics, edited by John J. Gumperz and Dell Hymes, 346–80. New York: Holt, Rinehart, and Winston, 1972.

Schenkein, J., ed. *Studies in the Organization of Conversational Interaction*. New York: Academic Press, 1978.

Schlesinger, Arthur M., Jr. *Robert Kennedy and His Times*. Boston: Houghton Mifflin, 1978.

Schrager, Samuel. "What Is Social in Oral History?" *International Journal of Oral History* 4 (June 1983): 76–98.

Schulman, Eveline D. *Intervention in Human Services*. 2d ed. St. Louis, MO: C. V. Mosby, 1978.

Schutz, Alfred. *Collected Papers I: The Problem of Social Reality*, edited by Maurice Natanson. The Hague: Martinus Nijhoff, 1967.

——. *The Phenomenology of the Social World*, edited by John Wild, translated by George Walsh and Frederick Lehnert. Evanston, IL: Northwestern University Press, 1967.

Scaraffia, Lucetta. "Marriage, Death and Nature." In *Our Common History: The Transformation of Europe*, edited by Paul Thompson, 201–9. London: Pluto Press, 1982.

Scase, Richard, and Robert Coffee. *The Real World of the Small Business Owner*. London: Croom Helm, 1980.

Searle, John R. *Speech Acts: An Essay in the Philosophy of Language*. Cambridge: Cambridge University Press, 1969.

Seldon, Anthony. "Elite Oral History." *Oral History: The Journal of the Oral History Society* 10 (Spring 1982): 12–14.

——. "Learning by Word of Mouth." *London Times Higher Education Supplement* 511 (20 August 1982): 10.

Seldon, Anthony, and Joanna Pappworth. *By Word of Mouth: 'Elite' Oral History*. London and New York: Methuen, 1983.

Sherrington, A. "Oral History." *Canadian Medical Association Journal* 9 (1982): 102.

Sherwood, Hugh C. *The Journalistic Interview*. New York: Harper and Row, 1969.

Sherzer, Joel, and Anthony C. Woodbury, eds. *Native American Discourse: Poetics and Rhetoric*. Cambridge: Cambridge University Press, 1987.

Shimanoff, Susan. *Communication Rules: Theory and Research*. Beverly Hills, CA: Sage Publications, 1980.

Shockley, Ann Allen. "Oral History: A Research Tool for Black History." *Negro History Bulletin* 41 (1978):781–89.

Shumway, Gary L., and William G. Hartley. *A Guide for Oral History Programs*. Fullerton: California State University and Southern California Local History Council, 1973.

Sitton, Thad. "Oral Life History: From Tape Recorder to Typewriter." *The Social Studies* 72 (1981): 120–26.

Sitton, Thad, George L. Mehaffey, and O. L. Davis, Jr. *Oral History: A Guide for Teachers (and Others)*. Austin: University of Texas Press, 1983.

Slettat, Dagfinn. "Farmwives, Farmhands and the Changing Rural Community in Trondelag, Norway." In *Our Common History: The Transformation of Europe*, edited by Paul Thompson, 144–54. London: Pluto Press, 1982.

Smith, Mary John. *Persuasion and Human Action: A Review and Critique of Social Influence Theories*. Belmont, CA: Wadsworth, 1982.

———. *Contemporary Communication Research Methods*. Belmont, CA: Wadsworth, 1988.

Spanos, William V., ed. *Martin Heidegger and the Question of Literature: Toward a Postmodern Literary Hermeneutics*. Bloomington, IN: Indiana University Press, 1976.

Speer, Jean Haskell. "Speech, History, and the Politics of Spoken Memory." In *Miteinander Sprechen Und Handeln*, edited by Hellmut Geissner, 289–98. New York: Scriptor, 1986.

Stewart, John, and Gerry Philipsen. "Communication as Situated Accomplishment: The Cases of Hermeneutics and Ethnography." In *Progress in Communication Sciences*, Vol. 5, edited by Brenda Dervin and Melvin J. Voight. Norwood, NJ: Ablex, 1984.

Stott, William. *Documentary Expression and Thirties America*. New York: Oxford University Press, 1973.

Stubbs, Michael. *Discourse Analysis: The Sociolinguistic Analysis of Natural Language*. Chicago: University of Chicago Press, 1983.

Sudman, Seymour, and Norman M. Bradburn. *Asking Questions*. San Francisco: Jossey-Bass Publishing, 1982.

Sudnow, David, ed. *Studies in Social Interaction*. New York: Free Press, 1972.

Susman, Warren, ed. *Culture and Commitment 1929–1945*. New York: George Braziller, 1973.

Sutherland, John W. *A General Systems Philosophy for the Social and Behavioral Sciences*. New York: George Braziller, 1973.

Swegman, Marjan. "Women in Resistance Organizations in the Netherlands." In *Our Common History: The Transformation of Europe*, edited by Paul Thompson, 297–310. London: Pluto Press, 1982.

Synge, Jane. "Cohort Analysis in the Planning and Interpretation of Research Using Life Histories." In *Biography and Society*, edited by Daniel Bertaux, 235–47. Beverly Hills, CA: Sage Publications, 1981.

Szczepanski, Jan. "The Use of Autobiographies in Historical Social

Psychology." In *Biography and Society*, edited by Daniel Bertaux, 225–34. Beverly Hills, CA: Sage Publications, 1981.

Tannen, Deborah. *Conversational Style: Analyzing Talk among Friends*. Norwood, NJ: Ablex, 1984.

Tedlock, Dennis. *The Spoken Word and the Work of Interpretation*. Philadelphia: University of Pennsylvania Press, 1983.

Terkel, Studs. *Hard Times: An Oral History of the Great Depression* New York: Pantheon Books, 1970.

Terrill, Tom, and Jerrold Hirsch. *Such as Us: Southern Voices of the Thirties*. Chapel Hill: University of North Carolina Press, 1978.

Thomas, Sherry. "Digging Beneath the Surface: Oral History Techniques." *Frontiers* 7 (1983): 50–55.

Thomas-Hope, Elizabeth. "Hopes and Reality in the West Indian Migration to Britain." *Oral History* 8 (Spring 1980): 35–42.

Thompson, Paul. *The Edwardians: The Remaking of British Society*. London: Weidenfield and Nicolson, 1975.

———. *The Voice of the Past: Oral History*. London: Oxford University Press, 1978.

———. "The New Oral History in France." *Oral History* 8 (Spring 1980): 14–20.

———. "The Humanistic Tradition and Life Histories in Poland." In *Our Common History: The Transformation of Europe*, edited by Paul Thompson, 313–21. London: Pluto Press, 1982.

———. "Life Histories and the Analysis of Social Change." In *Biography and Society: The Life History Approach in the Social Sciences*, edited by Daniel Bertaux, 289–306. Beverly Hills, CA: Sage Publications, 1981.

———. "Oral History and the Historian." *History Today* 33 (June 1983): 24–28.

———, ed. *Our Common History: The Transformation of Europe*. London: Pluto Press, 1982.

Thompson, Paul, and Joanna Bornat. "Interview with Stephen Peat." *Oral History: The Journal of the Oral History Society* (Spring 1982): 47–55.

Tilly, A. "History as Told." *Review* 65, no. 2 (1981): 18–21.

Tilly, Louise A. "People's History and Social Science History." *Social Science History* 7 (Fall 1983): 457–74.

Tonkin, Elizabeth. "Steps to the Redefinition of Oral History: Examples From Africa." *Social History* 7 (1982): 329–35.

Toulmin, Stephen. *The Uses of Argument*. London: Cambridge University Press, 1958.

———. "Rules and Their Relevance for Understanding Human Behavior." In *Understanding Other Persons*, edited by Theodore Mischel, 185–215. Totowa, NJ: Rowman and Littlefield, 1974.

Tracy, K. "On Getting the Point: Distinguishing 'Issues' from 'Events,' An Aspect of Conversational Coherence." In *Communication Yearbook* 5, edited by M. Burgoon, 279–301. New Brunswick, NJ: Transaction, 1982.

Treleven, Dale E. "Oral History, Audio Technology, and the Tape System." *International Journal of Oral History* 2 (1981): 26–45.

van Dijk, T. A. *Studies in the Pragmatics of Discourse*. The Hague: Mouton, 1981.

———. *News as Discourse*. Hillsdale, NJ: Lawrence Erlbaum, 1988.

———, ed. *A Handbook of Discourse Analysis*. 3 vols. London: Academic Press, 1985.

van Dijk, T. A., and Walter Kintsch. *Strategies of Discourse Comprehension*. New York: Academic Press, 1983.

Vansina, Jan. *Oral Tradition: A Study in Historical Methodology*. London: Routledge and Kegan Paul, 1965.

———. *Oral Tradition as History*. Madison, WI: The University of Wisconsin Press, 1985.

Vico, Giambattista. *The New Science of Vico*. Translated by T. G. Bergin and M. H. Fisch. Ithaca, NY: Cornell University Press, 1948.

von Cranach, Mario, and Roman Harre, eds. *The Analysis of Action: Recent Theoretical and Empirical Advances*. Cambridge: Cambridge University Press, 1982.

Warren, Stafford. Recorded interview by Ronald J. Grele, 7 June 1966, pp. 29–34. John F. Kennedy Library Oral History Program, Boston.

Waserman, Manfred. *Bibliography on Oral History*. Rev. ed. New York: Oral History Association, 1975.

Watzlawick, Paul, Janet Beavin, and Don D. Jackson. *Pragmatics of Human Communication*. New York: W. W. Norton, 1967.

Wax, Rosalie. *Doing Fieldwork: Warnings and Advice*. Chicago: University of Chicago Press, 1971.

Webb, Beatrice. "On Interviewing." *International Journal of Oral History* 2 (1981): 128–31.

Weimann, J. M. "Effects of Laboratory Videotaping Procedures on Selected Conversation Behaviors." *Human Communication Research* 7 (1981): 302–11.

Werner, Oswald, and G. Mark Schoepfle. *Systematic Fieldwork: Foundations of Ethnography and Interviewing*. Beverly Hills, CA: Sage Publications, 1986.

White, Jerry. *Rothschild Buildings: Life in an East End Tenement Block, 1887–1920*. London: Routledge and Kegan Paul, 1980.

Wierling, Dorothee. "Women Domestic Servants in Germany at the Turn of the Century." *Oral History* 10 (Autumn 1982): 47–57.

Wigginton, Eliot, ed. *The Fox Fire Book*. Garden City, NY: Doubleday, 1972.

Wilbur, Martin C. "Reflections on the Value of Oral History in Chinese Historiography." In *Proceedings of the International Conference on Sinology, Section on History and Archeology*, 1980: 1073–102.

Wilke, Gerhard. "Houses and People in a Village in Interwar Germany." In *Our Common History: The Transformation of Europe*, edited by Paul Thompson, 126–42. London: Pluto Press, 1982.

Wilkie, James W. *Elitelore*. Los Angeles, CA: Latin American Center, 1973.

Wilkie, James W., and Edna Monzon De Wilkie. "Dimensions of Elitelore: An Oral History Questionnaire." *Journal of Latin American Lore* 1 (1975): 79–101.

Williams, Frederick. *Technology and Communication Behavior*. Belmont, CA: Wadsworth, 1987.

Williams, Michael. "The Microphone: Essential Tool for Oral Historians." *International Journal of Oral History* 4 (June 1983): 123–26.

Williams, T. Harry. *Huey Long*. New York: Alfred A. Knopf, 1969.

Wilson, Leonard. Recorded interview by E. Culpepper Clark, June 1976, Department of Speech Communication, University of Alabama.

Winkler, Karen J. "Sensitive Issues Pose Special Problems for Oral Historians." *The Chronicle of Higher Education* 27 (12 October 1983): 6.

Wolfe, Thomas W. Recorded interview by William W. Moss, 30 October 1970. John F. Kennedy Library Oral History Program, Boston.

Woodward, Ken, and Robert Coles. "Survival Drill in the Suburbs: The Cold, Tough World of the Affluent Family." *Psychology Today* 6 (November 1975): 67–78.

Yocum, Margaret R. "Family Folklore and Oral History Interviews: Strategies for Introducing a Project to One's Own Relatives." *Western Folklore* 41 (October 1982): 251–74.

Zuckermen, Harriet. *Scientific Elite: Nobel Laureates in the United States*. New York: Free Press, 1977.

Index

Discourse analysis, *continued*
  eration and coherence, 24–25; defined by Stubbs, 25–26; and substantive illocutionary acts, 42; and purposive behavior, 44
Disputability of events: and hermeneutical conversation, 65–66
Disputable assertion, 55, 57, 61–67, 69, 70–75, 77–78; defined, 131

Ebeling, G., 4
Editing, xvii, 116–18
Elite: interviewing, xi; defined by Wilkie, xiv; oral history, 25; oral history discourse, 26; informants, 30; defined, 131
Elite oral history interview talk: and topic management, 33–34
Embedded request, 50–51
Embedded story, 93–94
Encounter, 7
Entrance talk, 89; functions of, 90, 93
Episode, 7
Equifinality, 109–10; defined, 132
Ethnography, 26
Ethnomethodology, xvi, 26
Ethnotexts, xiii
Evaluation. *See* Story
Extralinguistic factors, 106; as analogic cues, 111–12

Face, 42, 65, 100
Face-to-face interaction, xiv, 8
Fanshel, David, 26
Fantasying, 16
Fieldwork, xiv; approach, 108
Fixed inscription, 14
Flexibility, 10
Flexible response, 48
Folklore, x
Formulations: defined, 43, 132; functions of, 43
For the record, xvi, 52
Friedlander, Peter, 114
Fusion of horizons, 7, 104

Gadamer, Hans-Georg, xvi, 4, 65, 67; new hermeneutics, 2–5; living speech, 11; hermeneutical conversation, 21–22
Generalized other, 107
Goal-action linkages, 11–12, 105, 129 (n. 24); and culture, 106. *See* Means-end relationships
Goal-directed, 15

Goal-related constraints, 18, 30, 80–81
Goffman, Erving, 26
Grant, 31, 46, 48–51, 55, 59–61, 67–78
Grele, Ronald J., xi, 5, 19, 64, 108
Grice, H. P., 26, 28, 100
Grossberg, Larry, 101
Gumperz, John J., 26

Halberstam, David, xiii
Haley, Alex, xiii
Harnish, Robert M., 26
Harris, Alice Kessler, x
Heidegger, Martin, xvi; new hermeneutics, 2–5
Henige, David, xiv, 11
Hermeneutical, xv, 2
Hermeneutical conversation, 19, 50, 57, 72, 77–79, 112, 132; as ideal type, 19; and cultural narratives, 19; Hyde's model of, 19–20; and contrariety, 21; defined by Gadamer, 21–22, 65
Hermeneutical relationship: between historian and respondent, 7; as a dialectical structure, 7
Hermeneutical situation, 2; and the oral history interview, 13; and the interviewer, the interviewee, and the historical event, 13; as synchronic and diachronic, 13; dialectical structure of, 19. *See* Structural constraints
Hermeneutics, xi; new, 23
Hermeneutic theory, 3–4
Hirsch, E. D., 2–3
Historian: as creator and user of oral data, 8; as debriefor, 100
Historical cognition, x
Historical event: and the oral historian, 13; and the respondent, 13
Historical evidence: and oral data, 7
Historical record: creation of, 5, 104; as an oral text, 14; and interviewer role, 102
Historical tradition: as diachronic, 13
Historical understanding, 4; traditional paradigm of, 2–3
Historicity: human, 3; of human experience, 4; of historians as interpreters, 4; of historical interpretation, 13; and conflict, 20. *See* Taken-for-granted
History, ix–x
Human behavior, 101; and choice, 105
Human communication, xvi, 97, 102, 117; in oral history, xvi; and intersubjectivity, 98; as a creative process, 101; as

a coordination process, 103; as a reason-based process, 104–05; and socio-historical context, 106; as an open system, 109; as developmental, 109
Hyde, Michael J., 19–21, 30
Hymes, Dell, 26

Ideology, x
Illocution, 29, 31; defined, 17, 132; and procedural constraints, 19. *See* Language
Illocutionary acts, 41, 90. *See* Illocution
Illocutionary force, 41
Imagined audience, 79, 100; defined, 14, 32, 132; and politeness, 42; and storytelling, 82; as recipient of stories, 90–91
Implicit communication theory, 11
Indirect request for permission to provide information, 48
Inferentially elaborative probe, 39–41, 66, 69, 74; defined, 38, 132
Informant, xiv; and story design, 100
Information elicitor, xv, 23–24, 32, 53
Information elicitor and assessor, xv, 54–55; and imagined audience, 56; and oral history conversation, 56; outcomes of, 56
Intended meaning, 3, 4
Intentional perspective, 105
Intentions, 103
Interactants, 7, 100, 110; and cultural rules, 106
Interaction, 8, 101, 104, 109
Interactive processes: of storytelling, xvi; of communication, 104
Interlocutors, 7
Interpersonal relationship, 8
Interpretation, xvi–xvii; of a historical phenomenon, 3–4; nature of, 4; in oral history, 4
Interpretational issues, 118; and video recording, 114–15; and camera placement, 114–15; and camera angle, 115; and camera operation, 115; and logistical concerns, 116
Interpretative acts: of thinking, 4; of speaking, 4
Interpretive communicative event, xv, 23; process of, 2; as rational action on the commonsense level, 16. *See* Oral history interviewing
Interpretive orientation: defined, xvi; toward human communication, 6

Interpretive rules, 27, 91. *See* Rules
Intersubjectively established knowledge, 14, 100
Intersubjectivity, 97, 100
Interviewee, x–xi, xiv, 5–8, 79–80, 102, 113; and topic control, 80; and goals, 81; and cooperation and storytelling, 90–91; and shared knowledge, 100. *See* Respondents. *See also* Informant
Interviewer, x, xiv–xvi, 5–8, 102, 110, 113; as information elicitor, 23, 25, 80; defined, 33; and challenges, 64–65; as elicitor and assessor, 79; and topic control, 80; and expectations in story production, 81–82, 89; as recipient of stories, 96; and interview control, 95; and shared knowledge, 100; and recipient-designed talk, 100; roles of, 102
Interviewer and interviewee relationships, 99, 112–13
Interviewing: as collaborative production, 30
Interview method, xiii–xv
Interview product, xiv–xv
Interview records, xv; and videotaping, 116–17
Interviews, ix–xi, xiv. *See* Open system. *See also* Episode
Interview situation: topical constraints of, 17–18; goal-related constraints of, 18; procedural constraints of, 18–19; structural constraints of, 19–20; and requests for information, 45; and single interviewer roles, 55; and dual interviewer roles, 56, 79

Jackson, Don D., 109, 111
Jackson, Sally, 26, 41
Jacobs, Scott, 26, 41
Joint construction of reality, 8
Joint creation, 8
Joint intellectual performance, 9
Joint intellectual product: interview as, 5. *See* Interview product
Jonas, Hans, 5
Journalism, x
Journalists, x
Joutard, Philippe, xiii
Joyner, Charles, x, 108

Kaplan, Charles, x
Kockelmans, Joseph, 13; on dialectical interaction, 22

Labov, William, 26
Language: as action, 17; in use, 26, 44; in oral history interviewing, 108; as content dimension, 111. See Performative. See also Illocution; Perlocution
Levinson, S., 100
Lewis, Oscar, 114
Life history, xiii
Linguistic possibilities: defined, 3; and hermeneutic theory, 3; and thinking, 4; and interpretation, 4; and speaking, 4
Linguistics, 24, 26
Lived-experience, xv; and the interview process, 4–5; of the interview, 8. See Lived-through experience
Lived-through experience, xiv, 33, 101–02, 104, 110; and risk, 12; diachronic meaning of, 13
Living speech, 14, 67; defined by Gadamer, 11
Locution, 17, 29; defined, 132. See Propositional level. See also Discourse; Speech act

McLaughlin, Margaret, 32
McMahan, Eva M., x–xi
Management: devices in conversation, 32; of topics, 32; moves, 43; and pragmatic coherence, 43; and usage rules, 43; and bracketing, 43; moves and co-operation, 47
Meaning, 103; corrected, 22; constructed, 23; new, 23; construction, 25, 44, 101; emergence of, 29, 112; and the oral text, 44; joint construction of, 48; as reflective, 101
Means-end relationships, 11, 105
Memories, 102
Memory, x
Message: content dimension of, 6–7; as propositional, 7; as relational, 7; relationship dimension of, 6–7; and sociohistorical context, 107
Metarules, 18
Methodological: assumptions, 30; issues in videorecording, 108, 114
Mintz, Sidney, x
Mitigated challenge, 55, 57, 61, 63–65, 75, 77–78, 112; preferred adjacency pair structure, 57; defined, 62; functions of, 62; illocutionary goals of, 62
Mitzal, Bronislaw, xiii

Morin, Francoise, x, xiii
Myth, x

Narrative: cultural, 19, 64, 65; and storytelling, 90–94
Negotiation process, 31, 90, 102–03, 112–13
Nofsinger, Robert, 26
Nonelite: defined by Wilkie, xiv
Nonsummativity, 109. See Wholeness. See also Open system
Nonverbal cues, 6–7, 62, 67, 90, 101, 112–13; and contradiction, 61; in collaboration, 91–92, 95–96; and context, 106; and videotaping, 108, 115; as analogic cues, 111
Norm: of politeness, 41; and face, 42; of interviewing, 112. See Metarules. See also Conversational maxims

O'Keefe, Barbara, 102, 107
Ontological primacy, 3
Open system: as a whole, 6; as synergistic, 6; as reciprocal influence, 6; and speech performances, 6; as developmental and evolutionary, 6–7, 109; and equifinality, 110
Oral historians, x–xi, xiv, xvi–xvii, 2, 107; and hermeneutic theory, 3–4; use of videotape, 108; and evaluation of oral data, 113–14
Oral history, x–xi, xiii; defined, xiv, xvi, 5, 132; new hermeneutics of, 2–5; as contextual, 10
Oral history conversation: Hyde's structural model of, 19–20. See Hermeneutical conversation
Oral history discourse, 2; as rational action, 2, 25; as naturally occurring data, 30
Oral history interview, x, 106, 108; defined, 30; process, xv; as an interpretive communicative event, xv, 23, 91; and storytelling, xvi; as a joint intellectual performance, 9; as a novelty, 12; as a risk, 12; as reason-based, 12, 14, 105–06; as hermeneutical situation, 12, 14; and topical constraints, 17–18; and goal-related constraints, 18; and procedural constraints, 18–19; and structural constraints, 19–20; synchronic features of, 23; diachronic features of, 23; as an open system, 12; as rule-governed, 30; and discourse analy-

sis, 44; and storytelling, 80; as a communicative event, 97; as a circular process, 104; and socio-historical context, 106

Oral history interviewing, xiv–xvi; as an interpretive communicative event, 2; constraints in, 2; creative processes of, 95; communication processes of, 97; as a reason-based process, 104; evaluation of, 114

Oral history interviews, ix, xi; historical understanding of, 4–5; interactive nature of, 97; roles in, 100; as open systems, 6, 109

Oral interview, xiii–xiv, xvi–xvii; as face-to-face communication, 5; as a joint intellectual product, 5; and meaning construction, 102; as process, 104; as synchronic diachronic, 107; as a negotiated, developmental system, 113. *See* Face-to-face interaction

Oral interviewing, xv

Oral interview method, 2, 117–18; and context, 67. *See* Interview method

Oral text, xiv–xv, 9, 104, 114

Orientation. *See* Story

Paralanguage, 71, 112; defined, 132; and pragmatic coherence, 50; as analogic cues, 111

Paralinguistic cues, 77. *See* Paralanguage. *See also* Nonverbal cues

Performance context: and discourse analysis, 25; and interpretation of speech acts, 47

Performance rules, 91

Performative: conditions of, 125 (n. 31); defined, 132

Performative level, 17. *See* Language

Perlocution, 29; defined, 17, 132. *See* Language

Perlocutionary effects, 41. *See* Perlocution

Perspective-taking, 100

Phenomenological social theory: of Schutz, xvi

Philosophical hermeneutics, x–xi, xv, 2–3, 23, 30; of Heidegger, xvi, 3–4; of Gadamer, xvi, 3–4

Philosophy, 24, 26

Politeness, 100; and elite oral history discourse, 42. *See* Norm

Preemptive defense, 61

Problematical, 20–21

Procedural constraints, 18, 30, 80; and turn-taking, 18; and role behaviors, 18; and cooperativity, 18–19; and illocution, 19; and propositional level, 19

Process: of oral history interviewing, xiv–xv

Prompt, 34–35, 55, 60, 63, 77, 125 (n. 21); defined, 34, 132

Proposition: and topic introduction, 31; defined, 132

Propositional level, 16–17; and procedural constraints, 19. *See* Discourse. *See also* Locution; Speech act

Psychology, 24

Putting off requests, 52; refusals and cooperation, 51–52; in the interview situation, 51

Question-and-answer complex, 116; of Collingwood, 25; and negotiation of topics, 45; as a negotiation process, 67

Questioning: as a mediator, 21; and conflict management, 21; and hermeneutical conversation, 21–22; and storytelling, 89

Raines, Howell, xiii

Rapport, 112

Rational action, 29; on the common-sense level, 15; and rules, 16; and imaginative rehearsal, 16; and ideally rational action, 121–22 (n. 36)

Reason-based, 104–05; and culture, 105–06. *See* Rules

Reason-based communication: defined, 11

Reciprocity of motives, 103

Reciprocity of perspectives, 98, 103

Reflective glance of attention, 21

Refusal, 48, 52–53, 55, 63, 72; indirect, 52; direct, 52

Rehearsed recollection, 33

Relationship dimension, 111, 113

Repairs, 26; in storytelling, 92

Request for clarification, 34, 48, 50, 60, 68, 72, 78

Request for confirmation, 37–41, 49–50, 55, 63–64, 66–67, 69, 71, 73–75, 77–78, 112, 127 (n. 45); defined, 35, 44; responses to, 44; of disputable assertion, 55; and articulated conflict, 59, 61; and mitigated challenge, 62; preferred, SPP, 58

Turn-taking, 18, 26; defined, 132. *See* Procedural constraints

Unchallenged record, xvi, 55, 100, 113
Understanding: as circular, 7–8
Uptake, 41–42; and embedded request, 51
Utterance: functions of, 31. *See* Speech act. *See also* Illocution

Verbal cues, 6, 62, 101, 113
Video recording, 7, 113, 117

Videotape, xi, xvii, 71, 108. *See* Interpretational issues

Watzlawick, Paul, 109, 111
Whole: as greater than the sum of its parts, 6, 109
Wholeness, 109–10
Wilkie, James, xiv
Williams, T. Harry, xiii

Zuckerman, Harriet, 114

STUDIES IN RHETORIC AND COMMUNICATION
General Editors:
E. Culpepper Clark,
Raymie E. McKerrow,
David Zarefsky

The University of Alabama Press has established this series to publish major new works in the general area of rhetoric and communication, including books treating the symbolic manifestations of political discourse, argument as social knowledge, the impact of machine technology on patterns of communication behavior, and other topics related to the nature or impact of symbolic communication. We actively solicit studies involving historical, critical, or theoretical analyses of human discourse.